Ten Years of Apparitions:

New Growth and Recognition of the Pilgrimages

Latest News of Medjugorje
Number 10
June, 1991

by
Fr. René Laurentin

Translated from French by
Juan Gonzalez, Jr., Ph.D.
Texas Southern University
Houston, TX 77004

Edited and Published by
FAITH PUBLISHING COMPANY
P.O. Box 237
Milford, Ohio 45150

The publisher recognizes and accepts that the final authority regarding the apparitions at Medjugorje rests with the Holy See of Rome, to whose judgment we willingly submit.

—The Publisher

Published by Faith Publishing Company
For additional copies, write to:
Faith Publishing Company
P.O. Box 237
Milford, Ohio 45150, or to,

The Riehle Foundation
P.O. Box 7
Milford, Ohio 45150

This book originally published in French as *"10 Ans d'Apparitions, Dernières Nouvelles De Medjugorje, #10,"* in June, 1991 by O.E.I.L., Paris, France.

Copyright © 1991 Faith Publishing Company

Library of Congress Catalog Card No.: 91-077083

ISBN: 1-880033-01-1

All rights reserved. No part of this book may be reproduced or transmitted in any form without the written permission of the publisher. For information contact Faith Publishing Company, P.O. Box 237, Milford, Ohio 45150.

TABLE OF CONTENTS

Chapter	Page
Publisher's Foreword	vii
1. Medjugorje is 10 Years Old	1
2. News of the Visionaries	5
Ivanka	5
Mirjana	5
Jakov	7
Ivan	8
Maria	10
Vicka	15
3. Ecclesiastical Investigations and Decisions: The Bishops Assume the Worship and Pursue the Study of Authenticity	17
An Inevitable Question	17
The Worship Assumed By the Episcopacy: October 21, 1990	18
The Silence of November 27-28	19
The Unauthorized Publication	20
Hic Fecit Cui Prodest	21
The Impact	23
The Meaning	23
Why This Ambuiguity?	25
Further Clarifications	27
Revision of the Ambiguous Text	30
Spiritual Conclusions	32
A Precedent: Don Bosco Unknown	34
Healings	35
A Hostile Silence	35
Those Who Give Thanks	36
Official Report and Thanksgiving	37
The Healings Continue	37

Seven Remarkable Files in the Course of Study ... 38

4. Polemics 43
   1. A Lull? 43
   2. The "Counter-Reformation" or the
      Wet Sprinkler 44
      Captatio Benevolentiae 44
      You Said: "Disobedience" 45
      You Said: "Propaganda" 46
      The Thesis 47
      The Method 50
   3. Michael Jones 52

5. Fruits 55
   The Visionaries 55
   The Parish 55
   The Struggle for Organization 57
   Growth of the Place of Pilgrimage 59
   Bishop Pilgrims 60
   Communities 61
      1. The Oasis of Fr. G. Sgreva 61
      2. About Tomislav Vlasic 63
      3. Other Communities 65
   Youth 2000 66
   Social Initiatives 69
      Prisons 69
      Childhood in Distress 70

6. Testimonies 73
   Mail 73
   Testimony of Sergej Grib, Russian Scientist 74
   Maria Gracia Masala de Cagliari 75
   Ex-Rock at Night at Krizevac 76
   One of the Numerous Vocations Born in
      Medjugorje 77
   An Expert on Spirituality Discovers the
      Holy Spirit 78
   An Alcoholic Anonymous Cured in Medjugorje .. 80
   Two Protestant Theologians in Medjugorje 81

Table of Contents   v

Fifty Deaf-Mutes on a Pilgrimage 81
The Healing of Nicolo Pacini on the Feast of the
  Immaculate Conception, 1990 81
Testimony of Fr. Abraham 84
Pilgrim Bishops and Words from the Pope 85

7. Messages 90

8. Conclusion 98

9. Documents 100
   Interviews of the Visionaries and Others 100
     Marijana Vasilj 100
     Maria Pavlovic 104
     Jakov Colo 109
     Marija Dugandzic 114
     Ivan Dragicevic 117
     Jelena Vasilj 121
     Ludevit Rupcic, O.F.M. 123
     Recollections of Fr. Jozo Zovko (1990) 124
       A Sign Requested and Received 124
       The Beginning of the Daily Rosary 125
       In Prison 126
     Léonard Orec, O.F.M., Rector of Medjugorje ...127
       1. The Pilgrims 127
       2. What Is It That Attracts Pilgrims? 130
       3. Pastoral Charge of the Pilgrims 135
       4. The Material Conditions for the Pastoral
          of the Pilgrims 137
       5. The Civil and Ecclesiastical Authorities
          Facing Medjugorje 139
       6. Medjugorje: A Good for the Church 140
     Assessment of Ivan Dragicevic's Trip to the
       United States 144

10. Chronology 147

Notes Outside of the Text
  Pilgrim Bishops in Medjugorje 87
  Persons in Medjugorje 88

ACKNOWLEDGEMENT

Thanks to all those who continue to send me documents, information, and photographs. They enhance these books.

René Laurentin
B.P. 808
91001 EVRY Cédex
France

PUBLISHER'S FOREWORD
SPECIAL NOTICE

Fr. René Laurentin authored this book for the initial French edition in June of 1991. In July 1991, the process began for the translation, editing, and publishing of the English edition, scheduled for November 1991. As we all know, drastic and radical changes happened in Yugoslavia during this five month interval.

In early summer, while the original French edition of this book was being prepared, Yugoslavia was facing the potential overthrow of its political structure, a confederation of republics mirroring the Soviet Union format. It was a natural follow up to the changes that a shocked world witnessed at that time with the overthrow of the Communist government in the Soviet Republics.

Like many of its sister republics of eastern Europe, Croatia declared its independence along with Slovenia. The Yugoslavian government faced dire consequences and possible civil war. The long standing disputes between Croatia and Serbia were about to explode again.

The subsequent events that transpired in the Fall of 1991 are not included in this book as the English edition was already in process. They provide a stark contrast to some of the events that took place in Medjugorje in late 1990 and early in 1991 as reported herein. An entire new face has suddenly emerged in Yugoslavia—one of war. It naturally has affected Medjugorje. We need to wait and see what time will bring as the story of Medjugorje continues to unfold. Obviously, the final outcome to the conflicts in Yugoslavia have not yet been determined at the time this book is being printed.

In the interim, we can only report on the existing situation as of November 1, 1991, and how it affects the events occuring in Medjugorje. It has become obvious that the situation is complicated, at times confusing, and that several different conflicts are taking place. First, the efforts of Serbia to destroy Croatia; secondly, atheistic interests to destroy Christianity and third, the efforts of the Communist government to prevent the Republics from achieving independence and freedom. It appears that Croatia is to take the blunt of all three movements.

At the time of this printing, it is also obvious that the secular press, particularly in the West (the United States), has failed to report what is truly happening in Croatia. There is speculation that the Serbian interests are intent on destroying Croatia's future by eliminating those traditions pertinent to Croatia's ability to survive on its own. Hundreds of Catholic churches have been bombed or destroyed. Schools and hospitals have been destroyed. Entire villages have been wiped out and atrocities abound. The loss of lives and property on both sides far exceeds what the secular press reports.

It is now suspected that Serbia, backed by the Yugoslav military, has attempted to confiscate as much of Croatia as possible before the inevitable intervention by the international community comes about. In the interim, devastation abounds. By mid October of 1991, Medjugorje reported that many thousands of Croatians had fled to Medjugorje as refugees due to the destruction of their homes or villages, or to flee the onslaught. The greatest haven of peace in the world has suddenly taken on a new perspective. Why?

As with the conflicts and reality of abortion, AIDS, chemical dependency, and the total breakdown of family life, the power of evil shows its ugly head in the conflicts in Yugoslavia. For ten years, no power has been strong enough to stop the apparitions at Medjugorje or to prevent the response of millions of people in their pilgrimages there. Could it be that Satan's last, desperate attempt would be in the form of actual physical combat and the destruction of the country? The answer seems rather obvious, given the experiences and history of Medjugorje during the past ten years. Still, SHE will prevail in the name of Her Son.

In the meantime, contributions to Croatia's plight are urgently needed. For those wishing to send donations for food, clothing, medical supplies, etc. please address:

Fr. Anthony Petrusic
Croatian Catholic Union
1, W. Old Ridge Road
Hobart, IN 46342

We see the events in Yugoslavia at present, as with much of the rest of the world, as part of the dramatic changes to a planet coming ever closer to its face to face appointment with its Creator. In one of the early messages from Our Lady at Medjugorje, she stressed that peace would never come about from the negotiating tables, but only through a return to God. She has repeatedly stated: "Pray! Pray! Pray!"

Bill Reck
Faith Publishing Company

Chapter 1

MEDJUGORJE IS 10 YEARS OLD

The apparitions in Medjugorje celebrated their tenth anniversary on June 25, 1991. On the threshold of this anniversary, in the autumn of 1990, the Yugoslav bishops had made plans to recognize the exemplary worship of the place of pilgrimage. The plan was so complete that it was recognized, *de facto,* on October 15, 1990. The President of the Episcopal Commission of Inquiry, Msgr. Komarica, officially came to celebrate the Mass at St. James in Medjugorje. In November, other Yugoslav bishops did the same, as we shall see. But the document, which had to state specifically and officially this *recognition in fact,* fell short and gave to the press the misleading appearance of a "condemnation," as though "there were nothing supernatural" in Medjugorje. This strange web will be unraveled in chapter 3. One often has the impression that the devil is interfering with Medjugorje. The word comes from the Greek *diabolos,* which means "divider," the spirit of entanglement and confusion.

According to some critics, ten years is a long time for a false apparition to last. But this rule *a priori,* which they established beginning with the apparitions of La Salette, Lourdes, and Pontmain, is unfounded. In the course of time, many visionaries have had visions throughout their lives. If the apparititions in Medjugorje are of long duration, it is in order to maintain this grace which is being threatened from all sides: from the Church and the State. It is like a "help to people in danger." But these extensions are especially necessary to give time for an education, a long pedagogy which bears its fruits. The tenth anniversary invites us to celebrate its successful results.

This deserves an act of thanksgiving because for ten years, Medjugorje, subjected to the imbroglio unceasingly renewed by the *dia-bolos* (who rages in the shadows), should have expired, deviated, exploded, but prayer, patience, obedience, loyalty to Our Lady, the commitment of intelligence and of creativity in the service of faith, were always the strongest forces.

One cannot imagine the amount of patience and of sacrifice on which this spiritual success rests. For example, in 1985 the priests of the parish were required to take some ten measures in order to stifle the work of grace of which they were the laborious and marveled servants. They wrote several leaders of the Episcopacy, concerned for different reasons, in order to submit to them their cases of conscience and to request a line of conduct (*Latest News* No. 4). How many answers did they receive to this serious letter? None. They were required to obey the order, dying inwardly...sacrificing the work of God and losing faith in the Church.

The amount of self-sacrifice (which is necessary in order to persevere amid such difficulties) is immense, and is clearly recorded only in Heaven. God, Whose work they daily see in souls, remained with them through the overwhelming task of the confessional, which was not forbidden to them, and they kept to themselves their daily unpresentable cases of conscience. Why did they not expose it at the time, when this secret problem was taking place?

In this dereliction, lived among so much opposition, they found enough priest confessors each day for the task (up to as many as 100). The sacrament of penance prospered in Medjugorje at a time when confessionals have become nearly obsolete in many churches. Thanks to them, Christ was able to generously continue His divine gesture of pardon which passed through the laborious listening and absolution of the priests.

What marvelous, deep, and lasting conversions take place in Medjugorje, which is undoubtedly a record for the number of daily confessions and the proportionate number of conversions. That alone would deserve an act of thanksgiving.

So many vocations are also born and are formed in Medjugorje at a time when there exists a crisis in vocations in so many countries.

This acknowledgment to God and those who have served Him is not an outburst of emotion, but justice and clarity. Simply stated, grace often falls short because man is to blame! At a time when people are losing faith and morals, including priests, when too many institutions become less rigid or deviate, it is comforting to see the work of God begin in Medjugorje, and elsewhere, and to create these environments again, contagious with faith and prayer. Why is it that many places are honored where the fruits are bad, but at Medjugorje, where such beautiful clusters are growing, it is the object of so much criticism from the most diverse and the most contrary horizons: from the right and from the left, from priests and from the laity. Even here, the *dia-bolos* gives proof of his genius, which remained with him after his fall and which sows confusion.

Christian realism, such as the responsibility to help persons who are being persecuted, has made me persevere in the service of Our Lady and dangerously risk my reputation. It calls me to continue, even today, the publication of these *Latest News* series, which follow a work of truth among strongly diverse false news filled with excessive fervor or artificial criticism from the masters of suspicion.

God continues His work with Mary, the Mother of Our Lord. She was there in the Gospel, at the beginning and at the end, at the Annunciation, at Christmas, at His first miracle, at the Cross, and at Pentecost. She is present in the spiritual struggle of our finishing millennium, for this work remains the place of struggles where Christ Himself has suffered, where every new work proceeds cautiously in its trial, where to continue doing good is difficult, where monotony is distressing and patience rare. After the excitement of the first surprises and of the miraculous ambiance of the beginning, Medjugorje grows deeper in prayer in the midst of struggles of conscience which are constantly renewed in order to discern God's plan. Yes, Medjugorje is a school of freedom. The Blessed Virgin does not dictate their behavior, even to the visionaries.

I said to Maria, who was subjected to many trials, who was uncertain where her life was headed:
— "For you, it is simple; you only have to ask the Blessed Virgin whom you see each day!"
— "But she does not present it that way. We are free, and it is up to us as to how we choose to lead our lives," Maria responded.

This answer greatly clarified for me what some of the problems and the daily successes of Medjugorje are for the visionaries (who have reached the age of making adult decisions), for the parish (torn apart between its spiritual aspirations and the turmoil of materialistic undertakings which the development of pilgrimage calls for), and for each of the pilgrims (who have to draw conclusions from the fruits which they have mysteriously received in this place of grace).

Chapter 2

NEWS OF THE VISIONARIES

The visionaries of Medjugorje are from 20 to 26 years of age on the date of the tenth anniversary. Why does one always speak of the "children of Medjugorje?" They were adolescents (16 to 17 years old, except Jakov who was 10) at the time of the first apparition. They are now full-fledged adults. Daily apparitions have ceased for two visionaries (today mothers of families): Mirjana, since Christmas of 1982, and Ivanka, since May 7, 1985. But the Blessed Virgin appears to them once a year: to Mirjana on March 18, her birthday, and to Ivanka on June 25, anniversary of the first apparition.

Ivanka

Ivanka has two children and is devoted to them. She had a house built in a rather remote area on the fringes of the village. She is protective of her family life and gently discourages visitors. I went to see her on Easter Tuesday, April 2. Before every conversation she warns me with a definite smile:
—"I welcome you, but let it be understood that I wish not to be asked any questions. I have already said everything."

Her life is in keeping with the popular Catholic tradition of the place with this generosity, limpidity, transparency which the Blessed Virgin has taught her.

June 25, 1991, she had her fifth annual apparition, on the anniversary date of the first one.

Mirjana

Mirjana is following a similar but more complex path. The only university student among the visionaries, she had lived her spiritual life in an atheistic environment. She has a dramatic perspective of the world today and copes with it in intensive prayer. She avoids interviews. However, she is less reserved than Ivanka, and shows a certain openness as a woman of the people, intuitive and intelligent within reason.

On December 8, 1990, Feast of the Blessed Virgin, Mirjana entered the hospital. On the ninth, she gave birth to her first child, Mary.

Her ninth annual apparition took place on March 18 at her home. She wrote the following information:

> "Five days before my birthday, while I was praying, I knew that Our Lady would appear to me at 7:30 p.m.
>
> "That evening many people gathered and we prayed. At exactly 7:30 p.m. she appeared; this time no light preceded her as at the time of her daily apparitions. She stayed for seven minutes. As she left, the heavens opened, and I saw three angels who attended her. It was only in August 1981 that I had seen some angels attending her like that at the end of the apparition.
>
> "This time she did not speak to me about the secrets. During the apparition, I prayed three Our Fathers with her: one for unbelievers, another for those who are in need of her, and another for the sick who were present. Then she blessed us all and all the religious articles which had been brought. I had many questions to ask her which had been given to me by other people. To all those who had asked for something, she gave only one answer:
> —*Pray every day the three mysteries of the rosary for unbelievers, and attend Mass, specially for them, once a month. God knows what their needs are; they must submit them to Him.*

And here is her message:

> *I am happy that you have gathered in such a large number. I wish that you would gather together often for prayer to my Son. What I desire most is that you pray for my children who do not know my love and the love of my Son. Help them*

to attain this knowledge. Help me, for I am mother to everyone.

My children, for a long time I have invited you to prayer here in Medjugorje. And I will continue because I wish that you open your heart to my Son in order to allow Him to come and to fill you with peace and love. Allow Him! Let Him enter. Help Him through your prayers to become capable of spreading peace and love to others because it is very necessary now at this time of struggle with Satan.

I have often said to you pray, pray. For it is only through this means of prayer that you will escape from Satan and every evil which comes with him.

I promise you, my children, I will pray for you. But I expect strong prayers from you, and I hope that you will spread peace and love as I have been asking you in Medjugorje for ten years.

Help me and I will pray to my Son for you.

On the second of each month, Mirjana has a communication with the Blessed Virgin. She prays with her for unbelievers; she receives at this time some locutions and sometimes a vision. But it is prayer which is the basis of these meetings.

Jakov

Jakov, whose departure for military service had been expected since the summer of 1989, has not left at the time of this writing, in spite of false news which unceasingly keeps coming up. He had served an apprenticeship as a locksmith, but never worked at this trade. In order to facilitate his coming to the apparition in the evenings, and to help him to go through the difficult stage of the end of his adolescence, the Franciscans employed him at the religious articles store at Medjugorje. But the tourist agencies were in search of visionaries like trophies which gild their coat of arms. For a time he worked for one of them at a higher salary, but that did not last. And the Franciscans took him back again at the religious articles store.

He avoids interviews and brushes them aside. Nevertheless, he agreed to a tour of Germany from February 22 to March 7, 1991. He was very happy with this new and superbly organized experience to the region of Regensburg.

Ivan

Ivan made two new trips to the United States—from October 24 to December 13, 1990; then from January 21 to the beginning of February, 1991. The Americans tried for several months for him to meet with President Bush. On his return Ivan is believed to have told several people, who repeated it, that he was able to meet him for 20 minutes on November 15. But this information, which seemed serious, was hidden or denied. When I asked Ivan to resolve between these two different versions, he answered that it was a matter of a private nature. The official version is that he did not meet the President, who had a very busy schedule. On the contrary, it is well established that he gave him a message (from him and not from the Blessed Virgin), and that he met three members of Congress, representatives of the President: Christopher R. Smith of New Jersey, Dorman of California (two congressmen), and a senator.

The meeting was then scheduled for the Breakfast of National Prayer on January 31, 1991. These breakfasts, where people eat a little and speak and pray a lot, are very popular in America. The one on January 31 had a national character and brought together 3,000 people, among whom were several hundred members of Congress. President Bush was present there at a table arranged in order to permit the best surveillance possible by the police. Ivan was also there but at another table.

It was on this occasion that President Bush asked the whole country that the following Sunday, February 3, be a national day of prayer for peace (not for victory). Representatives from several countries, including the Soviet Union, had been invited. An Iraqi spoke of peace.

One of the ecumenical prayer meetings which were held on that Sunday on the west coast included Muslims.

President Bush asked again for three days of prayer at the end of the war, without anyone being able to say whether Medjugorje played a role in this decision. The President, a man of prayer, is of the Protestant faith.

Congressman Charles Smith, who was one of the organizers, sent Ivan a letter on February 25 to thank him for his services during his stay in Washington, from Thursday, January 31, to Tuesday, February 5. On January 31, after the famous breakfast, Ivan was invited to a reception in the House of Representatives. A dozen of them and many more members of their staffs heard him speak for two hours on the messages of Our Lady. He answered their interested or skeptical questions:

> "You have shown a good deal of humility and candor [...]. You will be interested to know that your service has raised a considerable discussion on Medjugorje," C. Smith wrote to him.

That same evening, Ivan publicly had an apparition at a private residence in the presence of some people. On Friday morning he spoke at the Breakfast for National Prayer at a Seminar of Young People. Present were 125 Christians of all denominations, the majority Protestants or evangelicals. Many did not know about the events in Medjugorje, and their questions were not favorable at all to the Blessed Virgin. One of them raised this issue:

—"Has the Blessed Virgin spoken to you of her other children whom she had after Jesus: the brothers of Jesus of whom the Gospel speaks?"

Ivan, who had not studied this question, was scarcely able to discuss it and to remember that the brothers of Jesus whose names are known in the Gospel are cousins, sons of other women. He skillfully pulled himself out of it, not without humor, by saying:

—"The Blessed Virgin did not speak to me about it. It is to Vicka that she has told her life. Talk to her. She is available in Medjugorje."

This meeting revealed the problem which many Christians who are not Catholics have in accepting that the Blessed Virgin can be the messenger of God today. "One can hope that these young Christians will discover that to honor and love the Most Blessed Virgin is not first a 'Catholic matter' " (concluded Charles Smith, February 5, 1991).

Ivan was then interviewed for an hour by radio VOA (Voice of America). This interview was then transmitted to Russia and the Ukraine by Fr. Victor Potapov. On Sunday Ivan met many priests and seminarians, as well as a judge and another Republican congressman, Bill Lowry, for a time of prayer and reading of the Bible, followed by the apparition.

On Monday, February 4, he met a group of women, influential in Washington, especially Mrs. Barber Conable, wife of the President of the World Bank. In the afternoon he was interviewed by the *Washington Times,* which published an extensive account on Medjugorje. The article reflects the official version: The meeting with President Bush was not able to take place, but Ivan had several conversations with his chief of staff, John Sununu.

Maria

Maria, who must protect her prayer life and her health, especially after having sacrificed one of her kidneys for her brother, schedules visits with the pilgrims each day about 4:00 p.m., without closing her door to her friends. She has many throughout the world.

She made several trips to Italy where she has many acquaintances.

Fr. Orec and Msgr. Hnilica, Czech bishop and confidant of the Pope, took her to the Soviet Union in October 1990. The trip, full of inconveniences, permitted the travelers to see the real Russia.

To begin with, due to the cancellation of a flight from

Bratislava to Moscow, it became necessary to travel more slowly by car to reach the Russian frontier. That enabled Maria to visit a Slovak doctor (a victim of 18 years of imprisonment). She had her apparition at his home.

On Saturday, October 19, to cross the Russian border, Msgr. Hnilica dressed in his episcopal dress with a pectoral cross and violet sash and skull cap. This helped him to pass in front of an endless line of cars. His luggage, filled with medals and holy pictures, received a benevolent inspection made easy by some presents to the customs officials. The time of the apparition was approaching. They entered the first little church which they found. Courageous people were reciting the rosary there. Maria told them:

—"Many come to Medjugorje from throughout the world, but less from Russia. That is why we have come to you."

On October 21, 1990, at Seredno, Msgr. Hnilica conferred the sacrament of confirmation to 170 people. Maria was moved when she saw a poor woman without shoes. She took her to a store to buy her some, but lo, there were none. In Mocassevo that same day, the travelers visited a church dedicated to the Coronation of Mary. Closed and abandoned for a long time, it had been saved by two little girls who had been inspired to go and pray there every day; other people followed.

On Monday, the twenty-second, in Uzzhorrod, county seat of the province of South Carpathia, a Polish priest welcomed them to his very poor residence. Since Croatian is a Slavic language, Maria, who is gifted, understood many things.

Finally, on Wednesday, October 23, they arrived at Moscow. The travelers were welcomed to a poor house, that of Michel, father of four children. He is in charge of the parish since there was a lack of priests. At 6 p.m. they had Mass at the only Catholic church open in Moscow, St. Louis of the French.

—"The lot of the world is not decided either in Moscow or in New York, but in the sanctuaries where one prays," preached Fr. Leonard Orec.

Maria's apparition took place after the Mass in the Chapel of Our Lady of Lourdes, to the right of the main altar, at the same time and with the same prayers as in Medjugorje. —"Now, it is Mary's time," explained Maria. "Even here, you see the fruit of the blood of martyrs and of prayer by all. The Gospa (the Blessed Virgin) undertook the spiritual direction of the Church through prayer."

That same day the travelers visited the Lenin mausoleum. The guards forced the bishop to remove his hat. That prevented him from taking from his pocket the miraculous medal which he wanted to leave in a corner near the lights which radiated the deified Lenin. But, is it not so that after having renamed Stalingrad, one hastens to do the same thing to Leningrad!

On Friday the twenty-fifth, there was a second Mass at St. Louis of the French, where prayer does not end. The people stay and continue. Fr. Leonard Orec invited them to come to Medjugorje, promising to find them lodging.

Maria and her friends spent a miserable night. On the evening before, a pickpocket had relieved her of her wallet with passport and plane ticket. It was then a race against time to have her picture taken, a new passport prepared, and all the necessary procedures to make the flight that day, October 25th, the day of the message to the world. It was on the plane from Belgrade that Maria received it. The word "peace" appeared in it six times, at the time when war was still on delay.

—*Offer your sacrifices and your good works for the peace of the world,* the Blessed Virgin said.

From the talks improvised by Maria at each of her stops, we present these:

> "Nine years ago the Blessed Virgin came to our parish as Queen of Peace. She asks us to pray for peace which comes from God alone: first in our hearts and then through prayer in our families. When peace has been established in our hearts and

in our families, then we can pray for peace in the world. The Gospa has asked us to live more as Christians, not to leave the Most Blessed Sacrament in solitude. She requested the formation of prayer groups, and many have been established."

Maria explains her own spiritual development thus:

"We were not children who prayed very much. We were like others, but we took the Blessed Virgin seriously, and we began to pray. The Gospa is guiding us; she has asked us to put God first in our life. Medjugorje is a school of prayer."

She stresses the simplicity of this teaching:

"Careful! When we are in church, we are good and holy, but outside we become pagans again. It is necessary to give witness wherever we are, even at school. When we begin to change, everything changes around us. The Blessed Virgin made us understand that evil exists. She has never said 'Do this or that,' but 'Decide for yourselves for good over evil.' She respects our freedom. She guides us as a teacher, but she loves us like a mother. The eyes of the Gospa which we see every day help us to enter into the depth, for they are blue and deep like the sea. Once we asked her how it was that she was so beautiful, and she responded: 'I am beautiful because I love.'

"Then we also decided to love more. She calls us to choose the way of sanctity. She has shown us that another life exists and the only thing that we can carry with us to the beyond is holiness. Several times she said: 'Now is the time of grace.' "

On her return from her pilgrimage, Maria thus summarized for me what had struck her:

"The Russians have an extraordinary love for the Blessed Virgin. During the apparition, many cried. In contrast to the pilgrims in Medjugorje, they do not ask for any physical cure, but only for interior and spiritual cures. It is a shame that many people come here as curious tourists. In the USSR I did not meet any curious people, but the people gathered for God and for Mary, eager for the meeting and the message. It is necessary to pray for those who do not recognize this grace. I met many people who had heard of Medjugorje without having been able to go there. This trip was directed by God beginning with Czechoslovakia, where many priests have spent 20 to 30 years in prison. Only prayer helped them to survive. The Blessed Virgin was very present to them.

"In the Ukraine, Catholics have recovered a number of their churches which were confiscated. They had become warehouses, some office structures, some museums. They were defaced. They cleaned them, purified them. They decorated them. These people are poor; they have only basic furniture. They have given carpets and little treasures which they possessed to revive their churches. Since there were no other places, it was there that we gathered, and at times it was the place of our meals.

"A large number of people were baptized each week. They are very active in asking for more freedom and to organize it. These people, who have been deprived for such a long time, hunger for God. For them, He is first. In Medjugorje, when I speak to some pilgrims, I at times experience fatigue, distraction; whereas there, the desire for God is striking: 'Lord, always give us hunger and thirst for You, us who do not know how to keep you in first place.' "

Vicka

Whatever the remarkable and diverse gifts of each one of the visionaries may be, she who has made the most direct spiritual itinerary in the most complete gift, without any interference, is Vicka... Even more, she offers herself willingly to bear the weight of the Cross for the cause of Our Lady's intentions. In previous volumes we have spoken about her trials and their objective, which she had announced beforehand. The other visionaries, whose itinerary is more varied in different degrees, are on a good path. But Vicka is ahead of them through a lucidity, a generosity, and availability without reservations to the pilgrims, which seems madness. How can one get through the day while being so put upon, and still maintain such unselfishness: her smile, her tone of voice, and this interiorness? It is Vicka's mystery. Very much in demand, she made several apostolic trips to Italy, then to the United States (January 11-28, 1991) and to France (February 8-10).

Her life has been a trial in several ways. She underwent three operations during the years 1984-1987 and, even more, mysterious sufferings which lasted three and a half years from the spring of 1985 to September 25, 1988 (*Latest News,* #7 and #8). She was completely cured September 25, 1988. In January 1988, the Blessed Virgin had informed her of the exact date. And this prediction was officially confirmed. Since then, her life, completely in the service of the Blessed Virgin and of Christ, enjoys a new strength and joy.

Her progress is remarkable in all aspects. From an impatient and choleric temperament, she has become patience itself with an unperturbable smile in a life plagued with constant obstacles so as not to know where to turn. One asks himself how it is that she does not crack up. One also admires the way in which she remains in control of the situation with purposefully good humor in the presence of so many pilgrims who engulf her with cars and lines of people, because each one wants to ask her a question, embrace her, take her picture, and obtain an autograph. It is crazy.

She puts everything in its place. Her unending enthusiasm in her progress toward God, her unqualified gift and especially her unequaled capacity to take on suffering while remaining a picture of joy and happiness, her forgetfulness of self and her dedication to others, compel such admiration. To that may be added her good humor and her knowing how to live, characteristics which one finds only among great leaders and certain countrymen, but especially among the saints. She is at the vanguard of the visionaries and of the pilgrims on the road to Heaven, but first, on the road to sacrifice. Certain members of her family follow her very closely in a very supportive way which also compels admiration from one who knows how to discern.

Chapter 3

ECCLESIASTICAL INVESTIGATIONS AND DECISIONS

The Bishops Assume the Worship
and Pursue the Study of Authenticity

Medjugorje has become one of the greatest places of pilgrimage in the world. More Communions have been distributed there than at Fatima: 1,373,850 in 1990. This same year, more than 30,000 priests and more than 100 bishops from the whole world have come in pilgrimage, often encouraged by the Pope.

An Inevitable Question

Yet, the Church has not taken a position. And this place of pilgrimage—rich in graces, conversions, healings—remains all the more controversial, as the bishop of the place opposes it. In April 1986, he had recommended his negative judgment to Rome. Rome refused his decision and transferred judgment to the Yugoslav Episcopal Conference, which named a new commission, at the beginning of 1987.

This Commission did not bring any light to the problems discussed because it was very secretive. I knew, however, that in the summer of 1989 it had practically finished its work.

Normally, the Yugoslav Episcopal Conference would owe its conclusions to the pilgrims for the good order of the pastoral. Actually, the criteria established by the Congregation of the Faith of 1978 invited the authorities to make a decision very quickly concerning the pastoral: put an end to the pilgrimages if there were some deviance, or be in charge of them and channel them if they do not present any serious objections and bear good fruits. In Medjugorje a pastoral decision was particularly necessary since the bishop of the place and the adversaries of the apparitions kept alive in the world press (which was misinformed) false news that the pilgrimages were forbidden and constituted a disobedience to the Church. This particularly troubled the conscience of people who had been converted through the events of Medjugorje.

But the much needed decision collided with an insurmountable obstacle. Each time that the question came up for discussion at the Episcopal Conference, the energetic and total opposition of the bishop of the place, Msgr. Zanic, did not even permit a clear discussion, much less a recognition of the worship.

The Worship Assumed by the Episcopacy: October 21, 1990

After a stalemate in the preceding discussions, a wise diplomacy move by Msgr. Zanic, obtained an agreement that the Yugoslav Episcopal Conference take charge of the pastoral needs, which could no longer be left abandoned. With this tacit agreement, Msgr. Komarica, President of the Commission of Inquiry of the Episcopal Conference on the Apparitions, came to Medjugorje on October 21, 1990, and celebrated Mass at St. James Church.

—"I come," he stated in substance, "in the name of the Episcopal Conference and of all the bishops, including the bishop of the place, Msgr. Zanic."

It was, according to the custom of the Church, a recognition of the worship of the place of pilgrimage. At Tre Fontane, Rome, nothing was done to recognize the worship established there to commemorate the apparition of the Blessed Virgin to Bruno Cornacchiola, a militant Adventist, who had planned the assassination of Pius XII (1947), and was converted by this apparition. That sanctuary, being maintained by volunteers, was of a private character similar to Medjugorje with a twofold difference: the diocese of Rome did not repress it, but closed its eyes; and the sanctuary of Tre Fontane was not, like Medjugorje, a regular parish of the diocese. In the spring of 1987, Rome decided to recognize the worship. Cardinal Poletti, vicar general of the Pope for the administration of his diocese, came to celebrate Mass at Tre Fontane. He did it without mentioning a single word of the apparition and without declaring in any way the supernatural or authentic character of the event. But this act of the Vicar of Rome constituted an official recognition of the worship.

On the evening of October 21, 1990, Msgr. Komarica spoke at length with the priests in Medjugorje in order to help them to assume the admirable but overwhelming pastoral task which they had been fulfilling for ten years. During the Mass, he had announced that his visit would be followed by that of other Yugoslav bishops, always in the name of the Conference. And that did not take long in coming.

From the fifth through the seventh of November, Msgr. Marin Stakis, auxiliary bishop of Davkovo, came, like Msgr. Komarica, to celebrate Mass and to preach an inspiring homily on the Blessed Virgin. On the seventh, he met the Franciscan provincial and the diocesan curia of Mostar.

From November 24th to the 25th, Msgr. Janko Spenesed from Siboca in Serbia, near the Hungarian border, preached likewise at the two large concelebrations of the Mass at St. James, and visited the site of the apparitions.

The Silence of November 27-28, 1990

Thus, everyone waited confidently for the statement which was going to make official this actual recognition of the worship. But the extraordinary meeting of the Yugoslav bishops held in Zagreb on November 27-28 did not produce any communique. The *Croatian Catholic Weekly,* which owed information to its public at the end of the meeting, received only this response:

"For the time being, we will not publish any statement concerning this session."

The *Weekly* consulted Fr. Orec, curé of Medjugorje, interested principally in the decision of the bishops. They received only this response:

"We, too, do not know anything [. . .]. We have not received anything yet."

On December 3, this article appeared in "Glas Koncila":

"The Institute for Marian Piety, dependent on the Faculty of Theology of Zagreb, has not until now studied the events in Medjugorje [...]. What would happen if an epidemic raged in some part of the world and the Epidemiologicla Institute did not react?" (*Glas Koncila,* December 3, 1990).

The Unauthorized Publication

On January 2, 1991, the Asca Agency published the confidential text under the negative title: "Medjugorje: The Bishops Conclude: It is not supernatural."

The secret text, having thus been made public, was preceded by a commentary from the same source:

"The presumed apparitions of the Madonna in Medjugorje, having up until now moved thousands of the faithful, do not have a supernatural character. Such is the conviction expressed by the bishops of Yugoslavia, where the famous place of [the apparitions] is found. They have sent to Rome, by secret ballot, their statement, which was approved almost unanimously (19 votes and 1 abstention) during the extraordinary meeting of the end of November."

Then the episcopal text followed:

"The bishops have been following the events in Medjugorje since the beginning through the local bishop, his local diocesan commission, and the Commission of the Yugoslav Episcopal Conference for Medjugorje. On the basis of investigations conducted until now, we cannot affirm that this is a matter of supernatural apparitions or revelations.

"And yet the constant gathering in Medjugorje of faithful coming from different parts of the world and motivated by reasons of faith requires the attention and the care of bishops. That is why our Episcopal Conference, in the spirit of ecclesiastical communion, is willing to help the bishop in residence to organize the pastoral work in Medjugorje in order to favor a suitable liturgical and pastoral life and thus foresee and prevent the phenomena and matters which would not be in conformity with the spirit of the Church."

Hic Fecit Cui Prodest

The bishops were disturbed with this unauthorized and untimely publication. Who then had seen to its publication? No one assumed responsibility for it, but it is the case of applying the famous adage: *Hic fecit cui prodest* (He who would profit from it, has done it).

The Catholic Counter-Reformation, the French community from the extreme right who condemned Medjugorje and provided the most constant support to Msgr. Zanic, openly praised him for this initiative.

"Vatican Radio announced on the twenty-ninth (December): For the time being no declaration on the events at Medjugorje will be published. It is thus that Msgr. Zanic, who one would say 'rallied' beginning on October 21 [an allusion to the statement of Msgr. Komarica], suddenly struck one of those decisive blows which he is known for. The report of the Commission of Inquiry remained a secret. Having been sent to Rome, this document in three points would be submitted to the deliberation of the Roman examiners who would reserve for themselves the privilege to publish what they would want, when they would want, if they would want, some day. Knowing that the conclusive document would never appear, Msgr. Zanic decided to reveal its contents by publishing it under the title: 'The bishops declare that there is nothing supernatural in Medjugorje.'

> "This publication is important [...]. Rome will be able to continue to favor the pilgrimages, but that will be an always more persistent lie. And yet the truth remains; it is most represented in this place by a single man; THIS MAN IS THE HONOR OF THE CHURCH; it is Msgr. Zanic. Some day he will receive the eternal reward from the Most Blessed Virgin: this pure mother whom he has loved so much and served with so much courage" (*Catholic Counter-Reformation*, January 1991).

Msgr. Zanic does not seem to have denied this reference up to the time of this writing. The numerous inaccuracies, with which the article of the Counter-Reformation is filled, and more ample information permit us to think that the publication of the Asca Agency was done not directly by Msgr. Zanic, but by his friends (Croatians and Italians, well placed in the Curia who have never ceased to support his action and who have become his Italian writers for the occasion). These prelates have done very much to create, in the Curia and in the press, currents contrary to Medjugorje.

In any case, the commentary of the Asca Agency, published following the Episcopal document, is a faithful echo of the arguments disseminated by Msgr. Zanic in the many stands he has taken (October 30, 1984, etc.). In fact, one reads in it:

> "In spite of the prudent expectation of the ecclesiastical authorities and of the Vatican itself, Medjugorje was quickly transformed into a place of continuous pilgrimages, spurred by the numerous movements in the Church, giving rise to an event in which theologians, bishops, and the faithful are passionately interested in and divided over, for or against the authenticity of the apparitions. Around the sanctuary and places of pilgrimage there has also begun a great mechanism bound to religious tourism" (Asca dispatch of January 2, 1991).

The Impact

This operation of the media found tremendous success in the press. Thus *Il Giorno* of Thursday, January 3, 1991, published:

> "The Yugoslav bishops: Medjugorje, no miracle. A hard verdict after two days behind closed doors. We must, they say, reestablish a proper liturgical life."

In similar manner, the *Corriere della Sera,* of the same day:

> "The Madonna was not in Medjugorje. Nothing supernatural in the current visions, say the Yugoslav bishops."

The same negative version from Vatican Radio (which gave a correction on the following morning), Radio Notre-Dame, a Belgian Catholic chain, and others.

The Meaning

Yet, the more experienced newspapers like *Avvenire* in Italy, the *National Catholic Register* in the United States where they asked me for my contribution, published a more just interpretation of this disconcerting document, and an interpretation founded on an analysis of the text. This document consists of two points: the first concerns the apparitions; the second, the worship.

1. CONCERNING THE APPARITIONS: The bishops considered it premature to commit themselves. Rightly so, because the cautious approach imposed itself on two accounts:

   - The apparitions had not ended
   - The 10 secrets are unknown

In the current state of the work, the "supernatural" has not been established, concluded the bishops. They took this ambiguous word "supernatural" according to the meaning used in a similar case: extraordinary, prodigious, miraculous. Actually, it is very clear that (supernatural) grace abounds in this parish and this place of pilgrimage.

The conclusion of the bishops is understood in reference to the two classic questions of rigidity in similar cases:

a. Is supernaturalness evident? Has the supernatural (the extraordinary, inexplicable character) been established?

And they answered "no" in the unfinished state of the events.

Since the first question remains thus in suspense, one normally poses a second one concerning the objections:

b. Is non-supernaturalness evident? Has the non-natural (illusory, diabolical, immoral, deviant) character been established?

The bishops did not pose this question because the answer goes without saying, since an abundance of supernatural graces has been given, conversions evident to everyone, and cures, already recognized by the Episcopal Commission of Medjugorje (*Latest News #9*).

Evidently, the supernatural has not been excluded, and that is why the Commission is invited to continue its work.

2. CONCERNING THE WORSHIP: The international scale of the pilgrimage, motivated by faith, involves the national responsibility of the bishops. They have thus decided to assume the care in this regard; they have offered their services "to help the bishop of the place," Msgr. Zanic, for a better pastoral measuring up to the pilgrimage needs.

And it is not a stray impulse, since three bishops had already begun this help in the most positive way.

This assistance does not consist in any way in helping Bishop Zanic to attain what he had been asking for since

March 25, 1985: "To eliminate and gradually suppress the facts of Medjugorje" (letter from Msgr. Zanic to the parish, March 25, 1985, *Latest News #4*). On the contrary, the three bishops who came to Medjugorje authenticated the worship of the place of pilgrimage. In summary, if one reads the communiqué independently of the partial interpretation of the Asca Agency, if he interprets it according to the norms and usages of the Church, if he deciphers its ambiguous vocabulary, if he refers it to the act of the president of the Commission of Inquiry who has taken charge of the place of pilgrimage in the name of the bishops, this document is simply waiting on the authenticity of the apparitions, but confirms that the bishops involve themselves in the pastoral needs of the place of pilgrimage.

Why This Ambuiguity?

What happened on November 27-28, 1990?

After clearly taking charge on October-November, how did the bishops come to this ambiguous and apparently negative text? The fact is that more than once at the time when one could not defer the decision any longer, Msgr. Zanic placed obstacles with the courage and vigor with which he is known.

Msgr. Franic, retired archbishop of Split, who several times witnessed these deadlocks, explained it thus in an interview given to *Corriere della Sera* on January 5, 1991. In confronting the fierce obstruction of their colleaue, Msgr. Franic explained:

> "The bishops do not want to humiliate Msgr. Zanic. When they pointed out to him [...] that there was no basis for his opposition, he began to cry and to yell *(piangere e a urlare)* and the bishops gave up insisting."

He succeeded in having the recognition of the worship (already approved) filled with negative things which he had expressed several times, to the point of becoming unintelligible.

1. ON THE AUTHENTICITY OF THE APPARITIONS: He obtained a negative expression: "One cannot affirm that it is a matter of supernatural apparitions or revelations." The negative is stressed by the equivocal use of the word *supernatural*. For the supernatural abounds in Medjugorje: a place for record confessions and conversions, where the adoration of the Blessed Sacrament has become constant. And Msgr. Zanic himself recognizes its fruits. To say that there is "nothing supernatural" would be equivalent to saying that there is nothing supernatural in the entire Catholic Church, of which Medjugorje is one of the highest and most remarkable places.

   "Supernatural" is taken here in the sense of extraordinary, prodigious, miraculous. But as far as this last meaning, let us recall that the Scientific Commission, overwhelmed by the number of cures (nearly 400 declared), chose two of them among the most obvious, and recognized their extraordinary and unexplainable character (*Latest News #7*, and *Latest News #9*).

   Msgr. Zanic also succeeded in seeing to it that the positive side of the uncertified report not be precise; namely, that the unrecognized supernatural is no longer excluded but still in a course of positive study. He arranged for the diocesan commission, which had been dissolved by orders from Rome, be placed on a footing similar to that of the Commission in office formed by the Episcopal Conference.

   All that rendered obscure the cautious approach of the bishops.

2. ON THE PILGRIMAGES AND THE RECOGNITION OF WORSHIP: Msgr. Zanic, who had tried so many times to have the place of pilgrimage banned, managed to get the new Episcopal document to recognize it in apparently negative terms:

   > The communiqué undoubtedly recognized the "motive of faith" which lead the pilgrims to Medjugorje, but does

not mention either the spirit of faith or the prudent, docile, and stable discernment of the faithful, or even the innumerable fruits, which even Msgr. Zanic recognizes like everyone else.

It passed over in silence the large and spontaneous "gathering of people," a criterion on which Msgr. Laurence (like others) established the official recognition of the apparitions in Lourdes. The gatherings of people in Medjugorje far exceeded that which existed in Lourdes since the official recognition on January 18, 1862, less than four years after the apparitions occurred.

On the contrary, Msgr. Zanic arranged for the worship to be characterized from a negative perspective. The bishops would seem to have less interest in cultivating a good tree than in pruning a bad tree. They gave themselves as a task to establish "a proper liturgical life"...as if it were not there, and "to avert or prevent phenomena and content not in conformity with the spirit of the Church." The bishops did not say that such deviant phenomena actually took place in Medjugorje, but the unilateral accumulation of pejorative terms allows one to suspect and support the anti-Medjugorje ambiguity, knowingly maintained by the adversaries (and intensified by the titles and commentaries of the Asca Agency).

Since all of these complications and anomalies have been given, one can understand why the bishops had decided not to publish their decision. The fact is that they were not proud of this communiqué, which was obtained for the sake of peace and quiet through a charitable understanding with respect to their colleague. They decided to discreetly send this faulty text to Rome with adequate explanations so that the Congregation of the Faith would further clarify the matter in a less heated climate than at Zagreb.

Further Clarifications

Further actions and information clarified the position of the Episcopal Conference. On February 12, 1991, in the absence of Cardinal Kuharic, the Secretary of the Yugoslav Episcopal Conference responded to Fr. Orec, O.F.M. curé of Medjugorje:

1. The Commission of Inquiry has not given, up to this point, any definitive judgment on the supernaturalness of events in Medjugorje.

2. The Yugoslav Episcopal Conference charged the Commission of Inquiry to continue its work into the future.

3. The Secretary of the Yugoslav Episcopal Conference did not give the press any opinion on the events of Medjugorje. He was surprised [of the unauthorized publication which had occurred] and asked himself how the information from Asca Agency could have been published.

Fr. Orec observed: "It seemed that certain circles were in a hurry to disseminate erroneous news in order to profit from it before the decision of the Yugoslav Episcopal Conference was known. All of this only creates confusion and thus makes a positive decision on the part of this same Conference more difficult."

As for the position of the Cardinal, Fr. Orec reported his significant statement:

"In an interview with Croatian television on December 23, 1990, Cardinal Kuharic, Archbishop of Zagreb and President of the Yugoslav Episcopal Conference, said that this Conference, and he personally, obtained a POSITIVE OPINION from the events in Medjugorje.

An interview by Radio Maria (Italy) stated that Cardinal Kuharic would have summarized the intentions and conclusions of the ambiguous comminiqué in three points:

1. On the authenticity of the apparitions, no definitive judgment for the time being, but the work will continue.
2. The Episcopal Conference has undertaken its constructive pastoral responsibilities in favor of the shrine.
3. It considers not to have concerned itself with the pending quarrels between the seculars and the Franciscans, an internal matter for the diocese of Mostar.

For the pastoral care toward Medjugorje, an appropriate commission of bishops was named, Fr. Orec clearly stated.

According to the telephone responses by Cardinal Kuharic to the German Catholic Agency KNA, reverberated by Asca Agency, the Cardinal stated in August:

"The judgment of the Episcopal Conference on Medjugorje is not definitive. The document remains cautious although its content has been published. Further judgment on the apparitions of the Blessed Virgin in Medjugorje will be given by the Vatican Congregation for the Doctrine of the Faith to which the Yugoslav bishops have sent these documents."

If this last observation is correct, it would confirm an evolution of Rome in these matters. Actually, up until now, the Holy See was careful not to involve its authority in this affair. If the Roman congregation makes a pronouncement explicitly on an apparition, it would be a novelty with regard to the traditions and customs of these last centuries.

In the same KNA message, the Secretary of the Yugoslav Episcopal Conference, Milovan, added that the message from Asca, although indiscreet, was faithful to the episcopal text. But this statement was only "the orientation of a moment."

Msgr. Frane Berke (Slovenian), Archbishop of Belgrade,

member of the Episcopal Commission of Inquiry on Medjugorje, who went there secretly once, stated a little more clearly, without departing from the official reservation:

> "It is not true that the Episcopal document of the end of November denies the supernatural in Medjugorje. The prelates wrote: the supernatural has not been established; but not "the non-supernaturalness has been established." The difference between these two formulas is enormous. The first cannot be interpreted in a definitive manner. It is open to further developments."

Here he pays tribute to Msgr. Zanic and to rigorous reservation:

> "This does not mean that I am favorable to Medjugorje. I maintain that we cannot give a definitive opinion. But there are signs in which, perhaps, there is or there has been something supernatural" (*30 Giorni,* December 2, 1990; *Eco,* March 1991).

Revision of the Ambiguous Text

On April 10, 1991, during the ordinary session of the Yugoslav Episcopal Conference in Zadar, the bishops revised the text of December 28, while clarifying the second point: taking over the pastoral responsibilities in Medjugorje. The changes are the following:

> The place of pilgrimage requires the attention and pastoral care, in the first place from the diocesan bishop, and with him other bishops equally, so that a holy piety toward the Blessed Virgin Mary according to the doctrine of the Church be promoted in harmony with it.
> To such an end, the bishops will also work out specific and suitable liturgical pastoral instructions. Likewise, the Commission will continue to follow and develop, through its members, the investigations concerning the events in

Medjugorje in their entirety (text published in *Glas Koncila*, May 5, 1991).

The changes are important:

1. They state precisely that Medjugorje constitutes a "pastoral" responsibility for Msgr. Zanic "in the first place" and for the other bishops.

2. The negative references to the "deviations" have disappeared.

3. The purpose no longer appears to be a vigilance against the repression of eventual deviations, but as constructive promotion of piety toward the Blessed Virgin.

4. The bishops commit themselves to the preparation of "liturgical-pastoral" instructions.

5. They invite the Commission to continue its work in order to clarify the supernatural character of Medjugorje.

These precise statements which confirm and synthesize the clarifications given by the Yugoslav Episcopacy since January have led to divide the Commission into two groups:

• One, theological, for the examination of authenticity.
• The other, pastoral, for the promotion of the worship.

In summary, the first point remains unchanged: "On the basis of investigations conducted until now, one cannot affirm that it is a matter of apparitions and supernatural revelations." One must understand, according to the context: "Up until now" the supernatural (in the sense of miraculous) has not been established.

The second part gives a reminder and clearly confirms the act by which Msgr. Komarica (and several bishops who followed him) had undertaken the responsibility and actually recognized the worship at the place of pilgrimage in Medjugorje.

Spiritual Conclusions

Dom Angelo, who disseminates the news of Medjugorje internationally in the different editions of *Eco*, has drawn spiritual conclusions from this matter, which has been needlessly complicated:

> "The relentlessness with which erroneous news has been published for years in order to crush Medjugorje, opens our eyes to the fury with which the demon considers his great Adversary who in Medjugorje snatches souls away from him and shakes the large number of Christians who have been numbed [...] with the sleep of death. He knows that his battle is lost [...].
>
> "But why so much adversity against Medjugorje?
>
> "Jesus too was condemned by the hierarchy of His times. Let us not be surprised if His Mother is not accepted either when She comes to Earth to repeat to us the Gospel message and to urge us to live faithfully. The Gospel opposes the tendencies of man who looks for his own glory and not the glory of God, even in the religious sphere. That is why he rejects the gift of God and the demands which it entails.
>
> "From it we have a double reaction:
>
> - Those who are willing to change their lives accept the call which leads to conversion.
> - On the contrary, those who are satisfied with themselves and who are content with an external and formalistic law do not accept the prophetic ways of conversion. They say: "The Gospel, we already know it... And it is a fanaticism or a mental derangement to eliminate. Let us be content with the daily events. That is more important than the extraordinary."

"But really, it is to this daily concrete and not abstract experience, lived with Jesus, that the Madonna calls us, and the extraordinary becomes necessary only because Christian people have forgotten the daily experiences. The Blessed Virgin is the prophetess of our times, and like all the prophets who came to remind of the demands of God, She is no more received in the Church Herself. Thus Jesus 'came into His own, and His own received Him not' (*Jn.* 1:11).

"Thus there is nothing to be surprised about [. . .]. Everything which is of God receives a similar welcome from mankind: contradiction, scandal, the Cross. But where the Cross is, 'I will draw all things to Myself,' said Jesus. This baptism is necessary for Him and for us. It is thus that Christ will conquer, for His power affirms itself in weakness (*2 Cor.* 12:9), and the Cross prepares the Resurrection [. . .]. It is when men increase obstacles that Mary brings about the greatest graces. We have observed it up to this day: each cold shower, each event brings about, as a reaction to it, a new interest and serves the expansion of the Good News. Thus in the beginning, the hostility of the government media helped to make Medjugorje known. Following that, the loud interventions of the bishop have always drawn more attention and, without looking for it, have eventually brought more water to Mary's mill.

"From now on, the stakes are down: through prayer, fasting, love for one's enemies, Mary has gradually gained ground to the point that the pilgrims, at first thwarted or only tolerated, are now protected by the bishops themselves. Such is the logic of the Gospel, for 'the folly of God is wiser than men' (*1 Cor.* 1:25). The Spirit guides the meaning of the faithful in such a way that they remain strong in truth, in spite of all the contrary sirens, and do not allow themselves to be snared easily by hairsplitting arguments." (Dom Angelo in *Eco,* February 1991).

From now on, no one can again say that *the pilgrimages to Medjugorje are forbidden!* They were recognized or assumed by the Church.

On January 2, 1991 (some hours before the publication of the stormy dispatch), Fr. Orec, spiritual leader of Medjugorje, concluded:

—"Medjugorje goes forward and ahead with the Church!"

A Precedent: Don Bosco Unknown

The surprising opposition of Msgr. Zanic to the apparitions in Medjugorje has astonishing precedence in the history of the Church, notably the opposition of Msgr. Gastaldi, Archbishop of Turin, to Don Bosco. While he was bishop of Saluzzo, Bishop Gastaldi had a great friendship for Don Bosco and regarded him as a son. When Pius IX named him Archbishop of Turin, then the capital, it was on the insisting recommendation of Don Bosco.

Bishop Gastaldi, sensitive and concerned over authority, was then transformed into an adversary of Don Bosco. For twelve years his opposition did not cease. He intervened against the final approval of the rules of the Salesian Congregation, then in the course of examination in Rome, where approval was nevertheless given as a final resort by the personal intervention of the Pope. Msgr. Gastaldi impeded Don Bosco's activity, suspended his faculty to hear confessions, and refused ordination to Salesian clergy. He spoke of Don Bosco as a man who is stubborn and violent *(testardo e quasi facinoroso);* he ended by influencing in a negative way the opinion of Pius IX. It was thus that Don Bosco was not able to obtain an audience with the Pope until the death of the later in 1878. Always under the influence of the archbishop, Leo XIII was poorly disposed toward Don Bosco. His letters were intercepted; again and again he was refused an audience.

Finally, the Pope found a humiliating solution to the conflict for Don Bosco. He had to write Bishop Gastaldi to ask him for forgiveness; this took a heroic act of obedience on his part after having undergone so much persecution. But Msgr. Gastaldi granted "the requested pardon." It was then that Don Bosco came to this conclusion:

> "In spite of the will to be strong and to remain courageous in adversity, by accumulating displeasure over displeasure, my poor stomach felt it was ulcerated."

Thus in the last years of his life, he was only a shadow of himself until January 31, 1888, when he died at the sound of the Angelus, at the age of 73.

As we know, he was beatified in 1929 and canonized in 1934.

Healings

A Hostile Silence

There is a sort of conspiracy of silence on the healings. The doctors remain generally discreet because of professional secrecy and because they do not like to talk about them before gathering all the evidence, which is usually lengthy. The recognition of a cure at Lourdes lasts some ten years on the average, sometimes longer.

On the other hand, Msgr. Zanic has limited his inquiry to investigate the sick who died after having gone to Medjugorje, where they had hoped for a cure.

The doctors, who were invited to participate in these inquiries, have been left outside at all stages. Professor Korljan, a psychiatrist responsible for organizing the scientific inquiry, did not sit on the Commission which was formed by theologians. The scientific work remained marginal. And meanwhile, the scientific inquiry presented a statement on the results, "as remarkable and entirely positive" on the mental health of the visionaries as well as the cures. One wonders why the communication of the Yugoslav bishops remained silent on this remarkable inquiry.

Those Who Give Thanks

Since the beginning of the apparitions, many sick have been healed in Medjugorje. They give thanks and at times Italian or American newspapers echo them. But oftentimes one does not learn about it except through rumor or by a chance meeting.

Last year I referred to two healings of certain credibility, since they related to doctors who were cured:

—Dr. Antonio Longo, an Italian pediatrician, whom I had met on the ferry, *Split-Pescara (Latest News #9)*, and
—Dr. Michele Espinosa from Cibut (Philippines; *Latest News #9*).

Their testimonies drew on the experience of a sick person who had been cured, and that of a scientific expert.

This year I heard of two other healings:

—Young Nicolas Pacini, 13 years old (December 7, 1990) of whom the Italian press spoke. The narrative appears here on p. 81-84.
—On April 2, 1991, in Medjugorje, I met, by chance, Heather Duncan, a nurse born in June 1956, who suffered from compression of the fifth and sixth vertebrae and from degeneration of the lumbosacral disks. Since April 2, 1986, she was able to walk only painfully with canes. She regained perfect mobility on October 2, 1990, after the Mass in English had ended and during Fr. Rupcic's prayer for the sick. She promised to send me documentation; it was a matter, it seemed, of a purely functional (and not an organic) healing, for if Heather moved with perfect ease (I verified it when I had her climb two flights of stairs in order to write a document), the condition of the vertebrae seemed unchanged, according to a certificate of October 11, 1990. That did not prevent her from giving thanks for being cured from her disability.

Official Report and Thanksgiving

It would be desirable for the Bureau of Official Records, founded by ARPA (Association of Italian Doctors) which opened its local office in Medjugorje on the occasion of the tenth anniversary, to establish a new typology for healings.
—Organic healings recognized as miracles, according to current criteria.
—Functional healings, sometimes more astonishing, when the function reestablishes itself without a healing of the injured organ.
—Finally, physical and moral healings, notably drug addicts, alcoholics, freed from destructive dependencies. It did not seem insignificant to us to point out some examples in each volume, including this one, in the chapter on Testimonies.

It is perhaps a pity that the (normal) concern for material evidence makes one neglect the experience and the benefit of the cures, for the benefit of only organic evidence. If it is legal to be overly strict with official records that have to furnish evidence, there is no place to close the spectrum of thanksgiving. The man born blind in the Gospel, who was not recognized by the scribes and never examined by doctors, still gave God thanks with all his heart and his thanksgiving still resounds in John's Gospel.

The Healings Continue

On September 26, 1990, Jozo Dalent, an electronics engineer, arrived in Medjugorje at the end of a long trip on foot from Ljubljana, from which he had left on September 21. He had undertaken this long trip of 812 kilometers (35 kilometers a day) to give thanks to the Blessed Virgin. For a long time a paralysis had impeded him from walking. He could only painfully move about for short distances with crutches. At the end of his first pilgrimage to Medjugorje in September 1989, he laid down his crutches, which he no longer needed. *(Eco).*

In his report of November 17, 1990, Fr. Leonard Orec

reported on the most serious cures of which he had knowledge in recent months. They are detailed later in this book. Besides Lola Falana, the celebrated singer from California (whose story we reported in *Latest News #9*), others include:
—Antonio Piras from Sardinia was cured at his home from a cancer with paralysis, when his parish priest brought him a stone from the hill of the apparitions. Italian television and newspapers spoke about it.
—Donica Anderson (USA) declared to have been miraculously cured of the results of an accident on the road.

"We received many other testimonies," concluded Fr. Orec. His rapid listing was an indicative reminder.

Seven Remarkable Files in the Course of Study

It is appropriate for all sorts of cures to be seriously studied for verification. To this effect, I remain in close contact with ARPA which devotes a significant part of its activity in Medjugorje. In January 1986, I had brought about the reunion of this Italian team with the French team of Professor Joyeux, and we established ten entirely positive medical conclusions which were communicated to Rome with ten theological conclusions concerning the ecstasy of the visionaries. A little later I had sent Dr. Frigerio, who began his investigation on the file of 300 cures which had been declared at the parish, which constituted a first documentary file. I repeatedly asked ARPA to furnish me the first selection of serious cures which had the chance of assembling a complete dossier (this became more and more difficult due to the complexity of medicine which multiplied techniques and desirable examinations). My requests have been in vain for a long time, because ARPA was in the process of setting up and became concerned over problems which medical confidentiality presents.

Charged with the responsibility of preparing a report for the occasion of the tenth anniversary, I stressed my insistence and I obtained a selection of some cures whose files appeared in good condition without involving ARPA. In this file, indeed in the foreground, were the three greatest and most documented healings of which we have already spoken:

—Damir Coric (Croatian) progressively cured beginning July 1981 from an internal hydrocephalus with partial cerebral destruction which appeared in a tomography; a case which was kept by Dr. Korljan *(Latest News #7)*.

—Diana Basile (Italian), cured on May 23, 1984 (while entering the chapel of the apparitions), from multiple sclerosis which had taken firm hold for 12 years and which had caused blindness of the right eye, grave motor disorders of all limbs, and total urinary incontinence (*Medical Studies,* p. 130-136).

—Rita Klaus (an American from Evan City), also cured from multiple sclerosis in eventful circumstances which we have narrated in *Latest News #7.* Having suffered since 1960, she was paralyzed. Tied to the use of her motorized wheelchair, she struggled furiously against the illness. She married and had children through Caesarian means for lack of motor functions. And she was suddenly cured on June 18, 1986, while calling on the Blessed Virgin after reading my book on Medjugorje.

Other serious cases (which I gathered from the parish registers) particularly caught the attention of ARPA:

—Kornelia Blatz, born September 14 1926, living in Oberbullendorf (Germany), suffering from recurring calculus in the right kidney and from contraction of the pyelourethral juncture (between kidney and bladder), was cured on September 14, 1983. She prayed while holding in her hands some of the dirt from the hill of the apparitions which someone had taken to her. In the examination which followed, further kidney calculus and obstruction had ceased. The flow of urine had become perfectly normal.

—Jasminka Burzic, born in Zagreb on October 7, 1982, with a deformation of the left leg, could walk only with difficulty and with burning pain in the heel joint. Her parents had not baptized their children and the father threatened the mother with divorce if she went beyond his prohibition. In July 1986, one of the child's aunts, Jasminka Vittoria Costci, was inspired to invite her to take her vacation in Otok in Dalmacia. She narrates:

> "At the beginning of July 1986, I invited my sister Stanka and her child to my house. I felt inwardly moved to invite them. They asked me to talk to them about Medjugorje. I did, and then I invited Jasminka to come for a bath. We prayed the Creed and the Our Father. In the bathtub I applied to Jasminka's leg some dirt from Podbrdo and I said to her:
>
>> 'It is the dirt from the Gospa. She will cure you. We must only believe.'
>
> Afterward, Jasminka was looking at the image of the Gospa and was embracing it. Then with her mother and her sister, she went to sleep at the house of her grandparents. On awakening she found her leg cured. She got up and ran to tell her mother; she was able to walk normally. Her parents were overwhelmed by this cure. They had all their children baptized in August 1987. The case is well reported since it deals with a congenital malformation which does not allow for subjective interpretations.

—Judith Ann Durrant was born on March 5, 1953, in Calgary, Alta (Canada). She had suffered from chronic myeloid leukemia. Her doctor, Dr. James A. Russel of the Tom Baker Cancer Center, testified:

> "The history of Mrs. Durrant began in July 1986 with a loss of weight and headaches. The examination of the peripheral blood (100,000 white corpuscles per cubic millimeter) and of the bone marrow,

led to the diagnosis of chronic myeloid leukemia [...]. From July 17 to December 4, 1986, she was treated by hydroxyurea and the leukocytes lessened to 11,200. She received a Busulfan treatment, but the control examinations certified that the white corpuscles were not normalizing; they varied from 11,000 corpuscles [slightly excessive] to 22,000 per millimeter.

"In November 1986, Mrs. Durrant went on a pilgrimage to Medjugorje and decided to stop chemotherapy. On her return to her home, she underwent the usual control exam, but this time the results were perfectly normal."

Since then, all successive controls have been normal. On April 26, 1990, the patient was personally interviewed by Dr. Antonacci who confirmed her perfect state of health after three and a half years of healing. She promised to send the required documents.

—Margaret M. Kondor, born June 15, 1923, living in New York, had been deaf for many years. On April 3, 1987, she was praying at the church in Medjugorje a little before 7 p.m. At the moment of the apparition she felt a tension in her right ear and two bangs in her left ear, and then she heard the priest's voice so loud that she thought that the microphones had been raised to a maximum. But she also heard her neighbors who were whispering. On May 4, 1987, she made her cure known to the parish and to Dr. Antonacci, responsible for the foundation of the Medical Bureau of ARPA in Medjugorje. She speaks now without difficulty and tests have shown a perfectly normal hearing. Her file is under study.

All of these sick give thanks. But the adversaries ignore them and repeat that there are no healings in Medjugorje. Likewise, the scribes in the Gospel were angry with the man born blind and told him: "You were born in sin" (*Jn.* 9:34).

Nothing has changed. Why is it necessary for the Good News and the signs of God's love to be so widely received in a despondent, scornful, or angry manner? That one should be slow and prudent before officially publishing the results is normal. But many of these Christians act out of fear and ignorance and close their minds in order to forget that God is good and that He communicates with us. How do we expect Him to communicate more if we are so prejudiced? Recognize God is good! Open your heart! Be prudent, but know how to recognize and joyfully proclaim the marvels of God as the Bible does. Share such recognition and joy with your brothers and sisters who are confused with the mercy of God.

Chapter 4

POLEMICS

1. A LULL?

In 1990 as we began the production of this book, we reported that polemics had run out of breath. It seems so.

—Msgr. Zanic has become more silent since his meeting with the Pope on February 7, 1991.
—*La Croix* withdrew from the polemics.
—The "scientific" volume announced by Belanger in 1988 is still pending.
—Michel de la Trinité, the most finicky and the most tenacious adversary of Medjugorje, left the Catholic Counter-Reformation where he was the number one polemicist. At a time when others broke with Abbe Georges de Nantes (particularly nine sisters and brother Laurent), he entered the Chartreuse monastery according to his vocation from youth. He began more than a year ago, and everything contributes to a good forecast for his journey.

Since I was his privileged target for years, I visited him at his hermitage, according to the precept of the Lord: "If your brother has something against you, go first and be reconciled with your brother" (*Matt.* 5:24). I did not come to discuss the polemics which he had abandoned for a higher service, but only to pray with him so that his high vocation would be confirmed. It is a severe test, for of 100 candidates who write to the Grand Chartreuse in order to request admission, only 10 enter and one alone perseveres. Everything is going well for Michel de la Trinité.

But since his departure, in the deprivation of complete poverty, he left an unfinished book to the Counter-Reformation, with the manuscripts of his articles already published. The Counter-Reformation, deprived of this combatant, uses the army which he left on the field. It edited his book in April, 1991:

—"We are putting the finishing touches to it," his successor, Charles Augustin de Saint-Sauveur, responsible for the definitive editing, announced in March. Michel de la Trinité did not participate in this elaboration nor saw the proofs, although his name alone remains on the cover. His situation, reconciled with the Church, restores an untouched quality to this conflict of the Counter-Reformation."

2. THE "COUNTER-REFORMATION" OR THE WET SPRINKLER

Captatio Benevolentiae

The polemic skill of the Counter-Reformation was genial, infallible in the art of the illusionist. The cover was skillfully titled, presented, and illustrated to provoke the fervent people in Medjugorje.

It is called *Medjugorje in All Truth, According to the Discernment of the Spirits*. If you love Medjugorje then, if you love truth, if you wish discernment (who does not wish it?), it would appear to be the book which one must read! One would not know how to make a better *captatio benevolentiae* (or more clever appeal) in order to make it read by millions of Medjugorje pilgrims. The cover is all the more assuring, as it is illustrated with a picture of the bishop of the place—Msgr. Zanic—and with a barefooted Franciscan on a pilgrimage to the hill of the apparitions. But inside the book, this calm image becomes contrasted between the good bishop and the rebellious Franciscans.

—"Msgr. Zanic will not cease to be elated as the destroyer of Medjugorje and courageous defender of the truth against the Pope, accessory to the "diabolical lie" (p. 502), the book states.

The Counter-Reformation stresses that the eulogy is reciprocal: the Bishop congratulates himself on their writings against Medjugorje (p. VII). "He regrets only our extremism against John Paul II," the Counter-Reformation observed. A euphemism for Msgr. Zanic adds: "I did not want to correspond with them [...]. They are against the Pope."

You Said: "Disobedience"

—"As far as the Franciscans, they have been stigmatized for their 'hardened rebellion' (from the Preface, p. VI)."

Paradoxically, the Counter-Reformation, which is at odds with the bishop of the place and which excommunicated the Holy Father, does not have strong words to be indignant at the so-called "disobedience" of the Franciscans. The book states they are "in rebellion against the legitimate authority of the bishop [...], in defiance of the holy discipline of the Church" (p. 247). Nevertheless, the Franciscans humbly exercise a regular and fruitful priestly activity in the parish where they are responsible without restrictions from the Bishop of Mostar. Would that the Counter-Reformation do as much, for curiously, all the terms which they use return like a boomerang against their community which persists in being at odds with *their* bishop. That does not prevent the Counter-Reformation from stigmatizing the two Franciscans from Mostar, who would have been considered competent to have administered the sacraments in Medjugorje in spite of the penalty of suspense which prevented them from exercising their priesthood. But it forgets to precisely say that Tomislav Vlasic and his successors, who fraternally welcomed these two brothers, forbade them to hear confessions and to celebrate (a weakening privation which was fatal to one of them). The Counter-Reformation does not practice the same obedience. Its book against Medjugorje illustrates an old paradox, well elucidated by the psychoanalysis of the Middle Ages: "Every man afflicted with a fault does not see it in himself, but accuses others of it." This phenomenon of projection frees him. This transfer, old as the world, has been well expressed through the slogan in old French of the Crown of England: *Honni soit qui mal y pense;* that is to say: He who accuses another reveals the evil which dwells in himself. The Counter-Reformation casts over the Franciscans (and elsewhere over me), with its rich make-believe, the insubordination which is its own.

The first pages appear reverently and quote some lines of mine with an appearance of objectivity (the reader must be infected with the venom without warning). It is much later that, little by little, I am gradually discredited, abused, insulted, with more and more pejorative words.

I was also accused of "formal disobedience" to the bishop. And yet, I regularly visited him, and I never disobeyed him. He fought and slandered me, but he did not forbid me to go to Medjugorje. When one of his communications seemed to forbid certain priests who were organizers of pilgrimages to celebrate Mass, I resolved the case of conscience in an orderly manner. First of all, I said to Cardinal Kuharic: "I do not organize any pilgrimages. I come for my research. I think that this rule does not concern me. Is it right?"
—"Ask Msgr. Zanic. That concerns him," the Cardinal answered me.
—"May I also ask him, on your part?"
—"Of course," the Cardinal answered me with a smile.

Then I wrote my interpretation to Msgr. Zanic, while adding obediently: "If I misinterpret it, I am ready to obey you."

Msgr. Zanic did not challenge my interpretation, and I am grateful to him. He fought me with extreme vigor, but he welcomed me and did not subject me to any interdiction.

You Said: "Propaganda"

The book is a potpourri of quotations which have been taken from here and there, from one source or another, with clear, incisive titles, appropriate to arouse the interest and to excite the passions:
—The undeniable proof of the existence of the Devil,
—the perjury of Fr. Vlasic,
—strong warning from Msgr. Zanic.
—John Paul II wants to substitute Medjugorje for Fatima.

—Rome reduced Msgr. Zanic to silence.
—The propaganda for Medjugorje is terrible.
—The propaganda is intensifying, etc.

Even here the Counter-Reformation is victim of the very phenomenon of projection; it is the Counter-Reformation which conducts the propaganda. It circulates its pamphlets and writings by the tens of thousands and appeared at the entrance to all my conferences to distribute them or to disrupt. But in Medjugorje, it is not propaganda; it is the grace of conversions which attracts. The Franciscans do not produce any propaganda. They preach conversion, fasting, prayer, reconciliation, according to the message of Our Lady in conformity with the Gospel.

The Thesis

This book, made of bits and dissimilar pieces, rearranges everything into three stages:

1. A very selective caricature which ceases in 1982.

2. The piece of polemic resistance (entitled "Discernment").

3. A "chronological synthesis" *(sic)*, which takes up again the caricatured skimming through in November 1982, in order to end with the Parthian shot, Rome's growing favor for Medjugorje—Rome and the Pope can only be the relentless supports of the work of the devil in Medjugorje.

This journey of loose pieces progresses insensibly with little touches here and there in three major stages which have been intermingled:

1. The visionaries and supporters of Medjugorje are ridiculous, unstable persons in rebellion against the Bishop, 'perjured" liars, and, what is more, "simpletons." Such are the epithets which one gleans from this development.

2. There are the "charismatics." Everything is charismatic in Medjugorje: Jozo Zovko. Msgr. Franic (a partisan of the apparitions), the visitors, and even the investigating

doctors: everything is charismatic, and the charismatics are the devil, as everybody knows.
3. Medjugorje, then, is the work of the devil; the prince of lies has established this subversive caricature of Fatima.

Paradoxically, the Counter-Reformation nourishes the ardent aggressiveness, not against bad Christians or even against the Christian left whom they neglect, but against the most traditional, the most praying, the most fervent Christians, because they are the competitors who take away from them their new members. For if the whole Church was progressive, the Counter-Reformation would gather all the traditional Christians toward victory under its banner. The supporters of tradition then are paradoxically the number one enemies of the Counter-Reformation. Their preferential targets are then at the top: the Pope (heretic and excommunicated), Ratzinger, Lustiger (the Counter-Reformation is much less concerned with Msgr. Gaillot). In this book it is specially Our Lady of Medjugorje who does not speak according to their ideology. This Virgin then is the devil, for to the military and political perspective of a victorious crusade in order to crush the head of the communists, Medjugorje dangerously substitutes for it a peacefull reconciliation through the conversion of all in charity. It is the abomination of desolation. Thus all the supporters of authenticity, including myself, are the tools of the devil. Such would also be the secret opinion of Msgr. Zanic (who, in fact, very often changed his opinion):

> "With respect to the satanic origin of the apparitions of Medjugorje, Msgr. Zanic has not always dared to affirm it, undoubtedly fearing that such a terrible accusation would raise against him the anger of people in Rome, defenders of their divine authenticity," one reads, and the following pages quote numerous plans of Msgr. Zanic, more or less favorable to this hypothesis.

The third part of the work, which follows, shows "the growing favor of Rome for Medjugorje," since Rome is for the devil in spite of "the firm opposition of Msgr. Zanic" (p. 431). In summary it states:

> "Medjugorje is [...] a total creation of Pope John Paul II [...], for without his indirect but efficacious intervention, the apparition, condemned by the bishop of the place in June 1982, would have immediately gone down in ridicule into nothing [...].
> "It is a shame for the Holy Church. An intolerable harm is done to the Most Blessed Virgin to tolerate, protect, and cause this pantomime to last [...]. Tomorrow it will be a terrible scandal for innumerable souls, so deceived by the negligence and the complicity of hierarchal authorities" (p. 501-502).

This dramatic quality ends with the last drama: the Yugoslav bishops condemned Medjugorje, but Rome and Fr. Laurentin have concealed it.

> "Fr. Laurentin deceived us, as is his custom [...] while observing:
> —If the supernatural is not assured, at least it is not excluded."

Fortunately, according to this book, Msgr. Zanic struck his last blow of audacity. [At the time when Rome was preparing to bury the decision of the bishops], for seeing that nothing public would ever come out, the courageous bishop decided to publish the essential material himself and especially the triple conclusion under the title: THE BISHOPS DECLARE THAT MEDJUGORJE IS NOT SUPERNATURAL. This publication showed the firm resolution of the bishop that no instructions of silence, be they from the Pope himself, would know how to constrain to silence the truth.

According to them, it was Msgr. Zanic who edited and published the unauthorized message from Asca Agency. But if the agency respected his title, which is radically negative, it would have sweetened the verdict of the Yugoslav bishops. He published only one tendentious, indeed, fraudulent version...

Through one of its con tricks, the Counter-Reformation transformed the moderate text of which the bishops deplore the publication but confirm the exactness. Since January, they have not ceased to reiterate: "The supernatural has not [yet] been established. The question remains open. The Commission must continue its work toward a decision" (preceding chapter). No! the text which was declared exact by the bishops, would be "fraudulent." They would not have only said: the supernatural is not evident, but it is excluded, so claimed the book by the Counter-Reformation (pg. 471).

My last lie, I suppose, is to interpret the text of the bishops according to its tenor and according to their authorized explanations, and not according to what the Counter-Reformation freely imagines. Laurentin "deceives us as is his custom" (p. 471) they state.

Thanks to them for playing so well, the role of the wet sprinkler—that succeeds in getting itself all wet in the process.

The Method

In order to correct all the errors of information in this book of more than 520 pages, one would need at least 2,000 pages. It is better to characterize the method by which this polemic drags the reader and practices magic on him through illusory evidence. The fundamental procedure consists in isolating negative elements (or appearances) from their context and to extrapolate them in the meaning of the held thesis, namely: Medjugorje is the work of Satan through the charismatics, condemned by the bishops.

The method is supported on two principles: one which the author states, and the other in which he remains modestly silent.

1. "The Church always gives priority to the examination of objections" (p. 197), declares the polemicist, concerned

to give himself some invincible weapons against errors.

That is a tough line, but not a rule of the Church. The Counter-Reformation uses, like a bulldozer, this destructive polemic principle against John Paul II as well as against Medjugorje. It casts heresy on its adversaries. Consequently, it considers itself responsible, in conscience, to condemn. One sees to what extremes the tendentious principle can lead.

Actually, discernment rests on the most integral perception of reality possible. A discernment is a diagnosis, not a dialectic. It calls for the most lucid and the most complete information possible.

2. The second principle which the authors do not state, but practice with conviction, is this: *one must discern without seeing in order to judge in every independence of judgment.* I know some experts outside of the Counter-Reformation (at least one, in the first two Commissions of Medjugorje) who were imbued with this principle: in order to be objective, the judgment must avoid all participation. Michel de la Trinité was intelligent enough to realize this weakness of the principle of the Counter-Reformation, and he would have wished "to go see" in Medjugorje, but "the Father" of the Community did not permit him. Regretfully, the polemicist stayed in a closed circle of objections.

He tried to destroy Medjugorje without knowing either the places, the milieu, the local culture, which is greatly misunderstood and denied in this book. From that we have enormous misinterpretations for him who has not seen or known anything: either the Franciscans, the visionaries, the sick who have been cured, the innumerable conversion. If Michel de la Trinité had been able to pray, converse, to hear confessions in Medjugorje, his polemic would have been affected by it. He would have even risked to change his opinion like Fr. Radogost Grafenauer S.J., the expert of discernment who was summoned by Msgr.

Zanic, and who was converted in Medjugorje.

Briefly, this book is a brilliant exercise of dialectics, powerfully oriented, where the analysis of these apparently negative elements, drawn from a vast written documentation, is treated with a spirit which hides everything positive and blows the negative aspects out of proportion.

I hope that these clarifications do not incite indignation against the Counter-Reformation. These are Christians and they are sincere, although passionate and taken in the trap of their ideology. May we pray for them as for brothers. I am the first to hasten to go to meet them as brothers, even beyond discussions as I did with Michel de la Trinité, since he laid down his arms. The love of neighbor does not require one to masochism, or to take risks under fire.

3. *MICHAEL JONES*

I will spend much less time on Michael Jones' new article *(Latest News #9)*, in *Fidelity* (February 1991, p. 16-27).

It is a very boring succession of hair splittings devised to give a negative meaning to the ambiguous text of the Yugoslav bishops, dated November 28, 1990, whose scope we have analyzed at greater length (chapter 3). Jones publishes this text in large letters and draws his own meaning with skilled tenacity. He puts it to work in the interview which he succeeded in obtaining from Cardinal Ratzinger. In spite of the requests and final touches (sensitive in his questions as in his transcription), it is clear that Cardinal Ratzinger did not give Jones his opinion on Medjugorje. He did not cease to repeat to him:

> Wait for the decision...Be more patient...Wait for the publication of the [final] report. All that will be more exact and more precise than it has appeared in the press until now.

Instead, Jones concluded triumphantly:

> The details can change, but the negative judgment [of the Yugoslav bishops] remains.

We have said with authoritative explanations in which sense this judgment was negative. According to the bishops, the authenticity of the apparitions was not established, but it has not been excluded. The bishops clearly stated that it is the object of an entirely open investigation.

Jones, who is known for his inordinate polarization concerning ecclesiastical sexual scandals, takes up his slander against a Franciscan who was supposed to have had a child in Germany. The ex-nun, mother of this child, has denied this paternity. To her detriment, she has left the service of a noble old man to whom she was a dedicated housekeeper, so they have associated this 90-year-old with this gossip. She regrets the false accusations which they have circulated under her name and would wish that they would leave her live her laborious and precarious existence in peace. I am shocked that Jones has been to harass this tired-out woman, on her return from work at 10:30 at night to try to make her say something, and that he had the effrontery to make fun of the broken German of this immigrant. Jones returns to it (p. 25). He seems to think that he is entirely right in his indiscretion, as in his scorn. He laughs at people and wants scandal. Let us leave aside this matter foreign to Medjugorje, which he works desperately hard to combine.

He complained that I cut him short in the course of the telephone aggressiveness which he showed me in one of the public telephones of the university where I taught in America. If indeed I interrupted him, it is that each time he seemed to take advantage of my answers in order to draw from them some kind of agreement over his slander, and he turned a deaf ear when I told him that he did not have the right to use this forced interview where I only referred him to my book. "I was nervous," said he. No, I resisted his aggression. I said everything that was useful in order to demystify the confusion of this polemicist. No one, not even Ratzinger, succeeded in escaping from this man, skilled in circumventing the speaker, in order to appear to have him say or to admit implicitly, what he did not say.

Yes, polemics is degrading, Let us not get stuck in it more. It is time to turn the page. Let us move on to reality.

Chapter 5

FRUITS

The chapter on the fruits does not cease to expand in spite of complications and oppositions which arise from all sides in order to turn attention away from this essential element, in spite of the recommendation of Christ Who gave this sole criterion on the matter: "By their fruits you will know them." (*Matt.* 7:16-20).

The fruits continue to exist at three levels.

The Visionaries

First of all there are the visionaries who were directly formed by the teaching of the Blessed Virgin. We devoted to them an edifying chapter: chapter two of this book. That the six visionaries have persevered in the faith for ten years in spite of the daily routine is a beautiful testimony. Not one among them has weakened; they are progressing each in his or her own way under difficult conditions of life in all respects. It is particularly significant at a time when the faith is disappearing in so many Christian families where fervor (remarkable where it exists) has become rare. The pastoral has widely abandoned the young people to the so-called cultural current which favors the abandonment to desire, sexual vagrancy, free union and abatement of religious practice. The testimony of the visionaries is a sign of hope. It has deeply touched a number of youth, as we will see later. For Medjugorje is not a sanctuary display window. It is not a matter of becoming excited over the ecstasy of the visionaries and the cures/conversions, but it is a call to actually live this same grace.

The Parish

During the first years, this grace made its inroads, like a tidal wave, in the parish of Medjugorje. If the place of pilgrimage has received much acclaim, it is that the parish itself has been an example of prayer, fasting, frequenting of the sacraments, seriousness in the faith, of welcome and hospitality, also of reconciliation, for the local quarrels among hamlets which were severe, violent, and even deadly, disappeared.

This was some event, an extraordinary adventure. Jozo Zovko, who does not have memory for dates or exact statements, but has memory of the heart, has given testimony to it during his most recent preachings. The event is probably dated August 5, 1981, according to another testimony cited in the appendix. Fr. Jozo told this fervent gathering, where there still remained many divisions and old rancors:
—"This evening, before beginning to pray, each one of you must pardon his neighbor."

The suggestion was received without protest. The people were ready for everything. But a heavy silence weighed on the assembly, for it is difficult to forgive and many were not ready. A great movement was brewing in the interim, discreet with some, but expressive with others, even to the point of tears. One of them ended the silence by crying out:
—"Lord, I have pardoned! I beg of You, forgive me!"

He perceived that this long rift called for a great pardon and purification on the part of God, and he was calling for it, according to the divine maxim of Christ in the Our Father, *Forgive us our offenses as we forgive those who have offended us.* He penetrated into the very heart of the teaching of Christ.

Today, Jozo Zovko stresses, with a rigor appropriate to the prophets, the crisis which has hit this parish: the economic and material development of the place of pilgrimage. Its hostelry, and its commerce (precious for these poor people who did not have another outlet than work in Germany and of long family separations) has transformed it into a parish-business, he said to them in substance. There is some truth in this remark. The business is exciting, including the pastoral work for the overworked priests of today. But the parish has kept the faith and religious practice even if daily Mass has become more rare and fasting has adapted to this overworked life.

In spite of taxes and constraints from the government which have persecuted the disinterested hospitality of the first years, the reception of the pilgrims in Medjugorje maintains, even today, a human, friendly, spiritual dimension. Many of the citizens have learned how to maintain in their homes or family boarding houses, which are not hotels, a family style where their testimony continues.

Medjugorje has formed an elite, unique in the world. It shows what it is capable of in the numerous prayer groups, and brings about hundreds of vocations in the world. These prayer groups, established and guided in part by the visionaries, are the model and the source of thousands of other groups which have multiplied throughout the whole world, as I have mentioned in previous volumes.

The Struggle for Organization

The apparitions in Medjugorje have been guided by an exemplary pastoral founded on conversion, prayer, and fasting, for an integral reconciliation of each with God, with oneself, and with others. The testimony of the visionaries and the support of an exceptional parish is the secret of the influence of which Fr. Orec, rector of the sanctuary, has given a remarkable account. We publish its essential points in the appendix (p. 127-143).

Its detailed statistics speak for themselves. The number of pilgrims has steadily increased since the beginning, in spite of so many setbacks and false information on the prohibition of pilgrimages. Medjugorje grew in spite of formidable constraints, and the problem of languages making the liturgy unintelligible for the majority. The density of the international crowd creates some more-than-uncomfortable conditions: long hours standing, and a lack of space, and facilities. All of that should have created disaffection, if not disorder and panic.

Fr. Orec, a wonderful organizer, was called back from Germany by the Franciscans to take charge of the parish of Medjugorje and establish order at this shrine which has become larger than Fatima, with ten times less its resources. He knows how to negotiate with the bishop who prescribed the "suffocation of the shrine." He established the first constructive relations with the Communist government. The first steps of the understanding were not the easiest; they demanded much patience and material and financial sacrifices. The government did not have the means to enlarge the access route, and the little narrow bridge over which the buses passed was dangerous without a guard rail. The parish covered expenses for improvements and thus knew how to create a climate of emulation and cooperation.

The Communist government had given or sold to some undesirables, amounts of land which were near the church and which were strongly desired by the local businesses. It refused, on the contrary, to sell this desired land to the parish, who wished to preserve a spiritual and religious area for prayer within a large perimeter. Everything that was in front of the church was irreversibly sacrificed and handed over to "Mammon." What was located behind the church was preserved. The school, which was confiscated and burned down by the government, could be repurchased. The fields which spread out behind the apse of the church have provided the space necessary for more than one million annual pilgrims. At the time when everyone was hastily building on the fields of Medjugorje, the buildings timidly begun by the parish were forbidden and the attempts at construction which had hardly begun were stopped.

Fr. Orec created additional space by repurchasing some shops to the left of the church. He set up a new presbytery for the numerous priests necessary for the service of the shrine; and housing for the sisters, who had lived for years under conditions entirely improbable and even dangerous, seeing the considerable and tiring work which they had to provide during the day. They had slept in a small room adjacent to the presbytery and in the belfry where the new carillon has now been installed.

Fr. Orec developed an area for the celebration of the Mass out in the open in the vineyards and woods behind the church. An esplanade was planned there. The old presbytery has been rebuilt. Space has been arranged for prayer and rest. Even bathroom facilities were built, which had been desperately lacking for more than five years (one has to think of everything).

Some reception and meeting places had been constructed to the left of the church where there is a chapel; perpetual adoration is being conducted there now, day and night. Outdoor confessionals were built which protected the penitents (and confessors) from the bad weather, indiscretions...and picture taking.

Some places, near the sanctuary, have been provided for the rising communities in which contemplative prayer and radiance are important, while waiting for a more permanent facility, for 15 communities are in the process of being set up in Medjugorje. There is a lot of work to do.

Growth of the Place of Pilgrimage

Accordingly, the place of pilgrimage continues to grow. The million communions were slightly more in 1989 (more than at Fatima). The statistics increased in 1990 when the number of communions surpassed 1,300,000.

Medjugorje has become a place of recourse and conversion for priests so often taken up in very external and sociological pastoral surroundings. They find there a spiritual renewal; 30,959 came in 1990.

—The English-speaking group is by far the most numerous in ever increasing numbers: 8,864 priests in 1990.
—The Italian group is next with 2,165. American pilgrimages have surpassed Italian pilgrimages, in spite of the distance, by 20 times.

They are also slightly surpassed by the Croatian group: 2,472.
—Then comes the German-speaking group: 1,789.

—Finally, the French-speaking group, especially Belgian and Canadian. Included are the forces from the right or the left, which had drawn scorn and hostility in France, against Medjugorje.

—The one which is growing more now (in spite of the lack of material resources which limits the pilgrimages) is the group from the East: 871 priests in 1990.

Bishop-Pilgrims

The bishops continue to come, more and more numerous, especially Americans and Italians (none from France), but also from the Philippines and different countries in Africa.

These pilgrimages by bishops are surprising when one sees the hostility of the bishop of Mostar who tried to substantiate, without a canonical basis, the prohibition of pilgrimages through confusion between what was official and what was private, contrary to the instructions of certain ideologists. Msgr. Zanic scourged these episcopal visits in his pamphlet of March 1990 with a publication of more than 50,000 copies in five languages. He stated:

> "I am particularly surprised at the lack of collegiality of some bishops (he complained). No one has the obligation to accept my judgment, but each one has the responsibility to study the events in Medjugorje according to his conscience before taking any position, especially if he occupies in the Church a function such as that of bishop."

In fact, the bishops who came did not do so without hesitation or information. They consulted at all levels (including the Pope, as I state later). Many go there in order to understand the deep and lasting conversions of the pilgrims of their dioceses. How can one ignore this living source? These reasons made them abandon the usual role of ignorance, dissuasion, repression, which is the most common on the matter.

Even when many official movements are in recession because of weariness or interior emptiness, Medjugorje raises a deep movement of fasting and prayer from which are born a large number of communities or prayer groups in order to cultivate and spread the unbelievable grace which Our Lady has enabled to spring forth in this place.

In each country, Medjugorje centers are born, especially for written or telephone circulation, or through telecommunications systems for the monthly message. In the United States, 173 centers have begun bulletins and newsletters. Many in Italy. Even in France there are many organizaions of this kind.

The organization of pilgrimages, forbidden to priests, have been multiplied by the laity: some hundreds throughout the world. These "nonprofit organizations" have no other goal than to permit those who feel concerned by the message to go and participate in the liturgical and spiritual life of the shrine under the best conditions possible. In addition, Medjugorje radiates well beyond the pilgrims to many Christians who do not have the time or the financial means to make the pilgrimage or who think that it is forbidden according to information which so many insistent Catholics circulate in good faith.

Communities
1. The Oasis of Fr. G. Sgreva

One of the significant fruits of Medjugorje is the birth of new communities concerned with fully living the message. Vocations flow in these young communities—at a time of crisis in vocations. And yet, the path of these communities is not easy at all (as detailed in *Latest News #7, #8,* and *#9*).

Fr. Gianni Sgreva has just cleared a hurdle. His community, Oasis of Peace, successfully left two dioceses where the project was not liveable (repression in the first; utilization and rerouting of objective in the second). They were then well received by Msgr. Nicolas Rotunno in Sabina-Poggio Mirteto, one of the suburban dioceses of Rome. They obtained their official recognition as a private association of faithful, according to the new formula created by the new cannon law of 1983: communities of consecrated life, open to married people, born in response to the new needs of the Church. The Oasis has a contemplative purpose with a ministry of intercession for peace, the object of a fourth vow, more than the traditional vows of poverty, chastity, obedience. It is indeed the whole essence of the religious life which this association of the faithful carries out, according to the less juridicial and freer character which the life of the post-conciliar Church takes.

The association was officially recognized on December 25, 1990 by Msgr. Nicolas Rotunno, bishop of the suburban diocese of Sabina-Poggio Mirteto. The rule was approved for five years *"ad experimentum,"* that is, for experience and eventual adjustment.[1]

The members of the community were already 52 in number by Christmas 1990 (12 novices); today there are 60. They established a third community in Medjugorje itself in the hamlet of Bijakovici, 300 meters from the homes of the visionaries. Six brothers and sisters settled there with makeshift means: three trailers and a wooden shack. The *Eco de Medjugorje,* had made an appeal to come to their aid: "Fr. Petar only assures them bread," the announcement stated. There are now some ten of them in joy and poverty. I visited them there on April 2, 1991. Another community has just been founded in Marienfried (Germany) and another in Circello (Benevento, near Pietralcina, birth place of Padre Pio).

The major portion is in the diocese of Sabina-Poggio, where I reestablished contact on May 19, 1991. The deal to obtain the ideal land ended in September 1990, in spite of difficulties which we have already mentioned *(Latest News #9).* If the funds follow, a first group will be settled before the end of 1991, and the rest of the community in the course of the following year.

FOOTNOTE

1. This official recognition was published in the substantial book written on the rising community: *Chiamati da Maria; Comunita Mariana Oasi della Pace,* Ed. Ancilla, 1991, XXXIV, 350 pages. Concerning the official recognition, see pages XIII-XVI.

2. About Tomislav Vlasic

Fr. Tomislav Vlasic encountered more difficulties. He did not seem close to obtaining the necessary authorization to establish his community in spite of the beautiful success of the Oasis of Peace, so similar in its purposes and its organization. But Tomislav Vlasic suffered a number of hostilities, calumnies, and unusual difficulties. He accepts these difficulties, as a true spiritual person. Thus he made the point to me at the end of 1990:

> We do not have canonical approval, juridical existence, or official recognition from the Church. We are under obedience, and I do not have any definite information to give. The community currently lives, not as an organization, but as a movement, in order to live fully and in depth, the message of Medjugorje. This project does bring about an attraction. The movement grows in the world. I receive many letters. We are late with our hearts. We have to guide, to help, and to form them. The plan of the Blessed Virgin is to develop this spiritual community in the whole world, more specially in the sanctuaries, so that these communities may be a living Eucharist. This project is understood with the heart, not with reason. It is a matter of developing a relationship of integral union with God in total abandonment. It must open up in depth. Without it, one will not go anywhere. It is a road toward mystery. We must not encase the sanctity which Our Lady of Medjugorje forms in the six visionaries. There are other graces and other gifts which God develops through the Virgin Mary. They are headed toward a spiritual deepening. It is appropriate to the dynamics of Medjugorje. It is important to be faithful to this dynamic which comes from God. In its absence we will become stagnant. It is not easy for theologians to enter into this dynamic. They often seem to be

prisoners of words and do not know what to do for life. The opening of the heart is essential, for the Word of God is the word of life and cannot be grasped except by the heart.

Tomislav Vlasic was officially the spiritual director of Medjugorje from August 7, 1981, until his departure (through obedience) in September 1984. He is cultivating the essential divine dimension of the Church. If the movement which he creates cannot find its canonical form, it exists as a movement. Many cultivate it privately, especially in America where groups are waiting for an official foundation in order to commit themselves totally to it.

The community, which was born discreetly near Parma as an experiment, has practically dispersed. A small group, which was in Bari (southern Italy) for some time, was transferred to Medjugorje but has left again for Bari to Fr. Pancrazio who has received them. Many of the members of the original community have become "external members." They live the spirit of the community in their previous residence in Medjugorje.

Tomislav Vlasic, whose services Fr. Orec knew well how to utilize, brings a stimulating participation to the spiritual life of the place of pilgrimage. We will find him again when we speak of the pastoral of the young people in which he plays a primary role. There, as elsewhere, he cultivates the spirit and spiritual formation (what is missing principally in the Church today). It is his charisma. That is what he brought in an exceptional way to Medjugorje from August 1981 to September 1984. This resource is important. But for that, it would be necessary for Tomislav Vlasic to end the long and unfortunate intrusion which made him establish this community on the charisma of Agnes Heupel. It is an entirely different vein than Medjugorje. Maria refused to join them, and furthermore, few are convinced of their authenticity. The fruits of this interference have been unfortunate in a prolonged manner (Maria's departure, disintegration of the community). It seems necessary for Tomislav Vlasic to free himself from this setback which has harmed his work and his person very much.

3. Other Communities

It is in this environment that other communities sprang forth. Fr. Luciano welcomed to Medjugorje a group of young people in search of a vocation.

In Foggia, Italy, where the archbishop is a regular pilgrim to Medjugorje, having recognized its fruits, a community was established. Here is the first information about it:

> After the experience of a retreat at Tocco de Casoria, a community desirous of a total consecration was born. It was lodged in a large house on one of the mountains near the city. Up until now there are only five members, from 20 to 30 years of age, but others are about to enter. Up until now the group has been only male. Some girls go often, but without staying there. In June 1991, a community life will also probably begin for them. In the house, the Most Blessed Sacrament is exposed day and night with perpetual adoration, as is the case in all similar communities, according to the experience of Medjugorje. They also recite the Rosary.
>
> To those who share this internal community life, an external fraternity will be associated with it on December 8. The bishop has verbally authorized it after mature reflection while reserving for himself the granting of his special blessing when the constituent act with its own regulations will be ready after explaining the activity of its members. These experiences are the fruit of the appeal from Mary to offer oneself for the world according to her plan of love.

It is in this same diocese that a prayer group of several hundred people was established several years ago. Under the initiative of a home environment, it met each week in the Church of St. Michael in order to respond to the calls of the Queen of Peace. Since January 1991, a proposition was circulated in order to better live prayer and fasting. It stated:

> "For five first Saturdays of the month (dedicated to the Immaculate Heart of Mary), there will be a nocturnal vigil for peace in the cathedral." The invitation was addressed by the Archbishop, Msgr. Joseph Casale, to all the faithful of the Church with the recommendation to give up the evening meal as a sacrifice for peace. The proclamation, in thousands of copies, circulated in the city and in the province.

Youth 2000

In August 1989, five thousand young people from the whole world gathered in Medjugorje from July 31 to August 6 for nine days of prayer. It was in response to the call addressed by John Paul II to the 500,000 young people of St. James of Compostela: to begin to walk with Our Lady and to become the burning messengers of the new evangelization, the builders of a civilization of love. It was in response to this appeal that *Youth 2000* was founded for an intensive realization in Medjugorje with the approval and support of the parish. This movement wants to be founded above all on prayer, and adoration of the Eucharist. It is a skeletal organization. The appeals from Abel Smith in the United States, and others elsewhere, want to promote a self-organization of young people in groups of twelve with a leader who would find priests to accompany this pilgrimage.

This "festival of adoration," as one has called it, was held under two immense tents, with a capacity of 3,000 to 4,000 persons, set up to remain near the woods behind the church. The young people came for the most part from English-speaking countries: England, Ireland, United States, South Africa, Sri Lanka, Singapore; and also from Germany and Austria, Poland, Czechoslovakia, Hungary, Italy, Spain,

Portugal, France, Belgium, Netherlands, Mexico, and Puerto Rico.

The heat was suffocating but the hearts remained attentive to the words of Fr. Tomislav who communicated his experience of the Eucharist. The instruction lasted from 9 o'clock in the morning to 1 o'clock in the afternoon with an interruption of only 15 minutes. The afternoon was devoted to adoration and to individual meetings.

Tomislav had immediately set very high goals:
—I demand very much from you because I love you very much.

He invited them to enter into the experience of the living Christ and the response was manifest day and night.
—Our whole life will be a preparation to welcome God, because that is the problem: we do not see, we do not hear, we are not ready to welcome the All Powerful God. Prayer should only be an opening to the Almighty Who wants to communicate Himself to us.[2]

Fr. Liam Loten, a young Irish Dominican, responsible for the music, knew how to create a climate of adoration and of praise. On Saturday at 4 o'clock in the afternoon, Operation "Throw Away What Stinks!" began. It dealt with open, radical confessions for which 50 priests were available. Then at 10 p.m. there was the vigil in darkness. The holocaust of sins emerged unto the illumination of a torch light procession around the church and, toward midnight, the celebration of the Resurrection.

On Sunday, August 5, after Mass, which was celebrated for each language group, the young people sang for the crowd until 6 p.m., the hour of the rosary.

At 10 p.m. it was the meeting on Mt. Krizevac. This tide

FOOTNOTE

2. There were conferences by Jozo Zovko, Philip Pavic, and Slavko Barbaric, all Franciscans.

covered the whole summit of the mountain. Some stayed there all night.
At the first light of dawn, the loud speaker broadcast the Rosary, lead by Fr. Tomislav. At 5:30 he celebrated the Mass. Be "the sign of Mary," he asked. Four large loaves of bread were blessed at the Offertory. One of them was distributed by a handicapped youth, hoisted to the top of Mt. Krizevac in his wheelchair in the arms of his comrades, along the steep and rocky paths. He had been chosen as distributor as a sign that everyone must share the suffering. The three other loaves of bread went from hand to hand.

— "I experienced the environment of crowds surrounding Jesus in the desert, hungry for His words and His Bread of Life," said Don Angelo Muti, member of the editorial staff of *Eco,* whose account I am summarizing here.

August 6, Feast of the Transfiguration, was the climax. The quality of the crowd is explained in part by the presence of a great number of young people who were already formed in spontaneous prayer groups throughout the world. This experience called for a follow-up.

Those who had not been able to participate in the festival at the beginning of August gathered in the same spirit from the 26th to the 29th of August, especially the Italians and Spanish-speaking (including Puerto Rico). It was the same tempo, the same atmosphere, the same awakening:

— Each morning, a half hour of adoration at 8:30 followed by a long instruction by Tomislav with a joyful recreation at 10:30.
— In the afternoon, there were Rosary, Mass, healing prayers.
  In the evening there was adoration guided by Tomislav who commented on "the Jesus Rosary."

Another meeting took place from the 25th to the 28th of October at Tocco de Casoria (PE, Italy).

On December 31, it was the vigil of the New Year, begun in the church of Tihaljina with Fr. Jozo Zovko. There was a long praying catechesis, in the course of which many discovered the gift of "slain in the spirit," a sudden and a total abandonment of the body and the spirit to God.

In the afternoon there was a preparation for confession.

At 7:30 in the evening, there was a climb to the hill of the apparitions, Podbrdo. That evening, Ivan had a prayer vigil followed by an apparition, as on every Monday. The vigil was anticipated that day and followed by an invitation to go to the church where the vigil ended in the spirit of joy and prayer for peace.

The vigil then continued at the church at 9:30 p.m. Slavko had all the lights extinguished and explained:

> "Darkness reminds us of the state of sin from which Jesus, Light of the World, became flesh for us, freed us."

Then it was a meditative Rosary, led by the visionaries Ivan, Vicka, Maria, followed by midnight Mass. The threshold of the New Year was crossed at the sound of bells and hymns. The songs continued after Mass.

It was decided that the festival of the youth would take place each year at the beginning of August. The request is urgent.

Social Initiatives
Prisons

One would not be able to relate everything that the message of Medjugorje inspires.

The evangelization and the regeneration of prisons continues in America (cf. *Latest News #9*). Msgr. Nicolas Rotunno went there in August from Rome to visit these prisoners. He was moved by their conversion and the quality of their prayer of the heart. Stan Karminski, who visited them in mid September, also had a deep impression. Many of these prisoners, on the way to being freed, look to the example of the Oasis of Peace, founded by Don Gianni Sgreva, as a close bond with the movement.

One of them, Jim Jennings, freed last December 15, after

three incarcerations of which one was for murder, rebuilt his life in faith in the service of the Lord. He works for the organization Queen of Peace Ministry, directed by Dennis Nolan, where he has discovered, with happiness, a new life.

Childhood in Distress

After the establishment of "Mepa" in Brazil (a home for street children), another initiative was born for children in distress in Bombay.

Mauro Harsch, the founder (in Italian Switzerland), thus narrated its origins:

> "I was a most lukewarm Christian who had strayed away from the Church. Thirsting for deep values, I went to Medjugorje in February 1985, on faith, after doing some reading. But before the pilgrimage, a dream imposed itself on my spirit: a large hill with a rainbow gave me immense supernatural joy. I quickly fell on my knees and the shock (though in the dream) awakened me with a very strong pain in my knees.
>
> "On February 19, 1985, I arrived in Medjugorje during very cold weather. Medjugorje appeared deserted and desolate. The church was cold. Some parishioners recited the rosary. I suddenly fell on my knees (as in the dream). I experienced then a love for everyone and an indescribable joy which I do not succeed in rationally explaining to myself today. Up until now, I had always refused to kneel down, including during the two days when my spiritual conversion began. I finally understood that God had to be the fundamental value in life.
>
> "On my return, my relations with others in daily and professional life changed profoundly. The idea came to me that faith had to be actualized in a vast work of charity. This plan turned me toward the children of the third world who die in great numbers every day. Thus, on December 31, 1987, the

Medjugorje Foundation for Childhood was born. It was officially recognized two months later and placed under the supervision of the Swiss Confederation. It collects funds for the young children and youth of underdeveloped countries, in direct cooperation with the missionaries working there. The Foundation is especially concerned with abandoned children and orphans, to provide them with housing, adequate assistance, sufficient food, medical care, an academic and professional formation which permits them to make a living in a manner suited to the needs of their region. The Board of the Foundation organizes cultural events to collect necessary funds. A patronage committee was founded with a variety of personalities, among whom were the bishop of Lugano, Sophia Loren, and film producer, Franco Zefirelli. The support is coming in.

"The Foundation circulated a film, the *Sisters with a smile:* Helpers of Mary, who work in the slums of the out-lying districts of Bombay, with only one objective: 'to foster, like the Blessed Virgin, a great love for the poor and the marginal, to love and help each child who is born, giving them the right to live.' The Foundation gave them the means to build an orphanage, the Villa Angels, which opened at the end of 1989. It receives 100 orphans up to the age of 18. I was moved by meeting with these children. I had never met any so loving, well raised, sensitive, and intelligent."
(Summary of the testimony from Mauro Harsh.)

The orphanage was built in Valiv, a village located 70 kilometers from Bombay. The house cost 150,000 Swiss francs. The monthly expense is 4,000 francs.

The second project of a villa for abandoned children was realized in Sao Paolo, Brazil, through the care of Guiseppe

Sometti, professor of the University, who left teaching in order to devote himself exclusively to the children of the third world with the help of European and Brazilian volunteers. One of the first objectives will be to dig a well of drinking water, which is absolutely necessary in the village, and homes which will house 15 children each, guided by adoptive parents. The plan is to build 200 of them for a total of 3,000 children, for it is a matter of removing them from hunger, misery, prostitution, drugs, and frustration. The children who are abandoned are at times sold, or disabled so that their begging provokes compassion, and the squadrons of death drag them away and kill them like rabbits.

One of the striking characteristics of the initiatives which have come out of Medjugorje is the voluntary service which assures their operation. That goes from the parishioners to the pilgrims who are in Medjugorje; from all classes, all milieux, even to a blood princess (from the imperial family of Austria) which assures a multi-lingual secretariat of very high level.

Chapter 6

TESTIMONIES

The chapter on the fruits concludes, as in the preceding *Latest News,* with some concrete testimonies.

Mail

I continue to receive letters which attest, in different ways, to the grace of Medjugorje. I will cite only a few and will give more space to testimonies of conversion, which form a horizon on the daily secret of the confessional.

> "Last month (August 1990), I went to Medjugorje for the first time for a one-week stay (August 13-19). Since then the distance which I have come is astonishing to me.
>
> "Since the age of 20, I had deliberately stayed away from the Church. I turned my back on it for more than 25 years, until the discovery of Medjugorje through a magazine, then through your wonderful books. I went there, well-informed but perplexed, with two ideas in mind:
>
> 1. Is this story really true?
> 2. If it is true, what is its meaning?
>
> "My stay was marked with surprising meetings, interesting exchanges. During the last two days, I even received, three times, the smell of perfume—of roses, it seemed to me. I experienced it in reference to the presence of the Blessed Virgin. It was perhaps the final gift of my stay, which made me fall over with emotion in my re-found faith. On my return to Paris, my life has begun again, but different from previously. I pray (not enough), I go to Mass, I listen to *Radio Notre Dame,* I give testimony (but prudently) on the exceptional event which I have just reported to you. The temptations

of Satan, the seducer, are not lacking. I am actively looking for a parish and a spiritual director." (A. L., Paris, September 8, 1990).

"With tears in my eyes, I left Medjugorje after a 3-month stay (June 22-October 14, 1990). It is like descending from Tabor. A 100-page notebook would not suffice to contain all the marvelous experiences lived or confidences received from so many pilgrims: the fruits of Medjugorje. Those which are repeated most often are peace and joy. Ah, if the numerous confessors could only speak!" (P. G., à S., October 24, 1990).

"I have gone to Medjugorje three times. One returns from it transformed." (E. C., à S., December 10-20, 1990).

"I am only a humble Christian whose faith, very troubled through anxieties which occurred during a certain period, in the bosom of the Catholic Church, has seen the latter brought back to life through a first pilgrimage to Medjugorje two and a half years ago. Since then I have been involved with the Parisian group *Etoile Notre Dame*" (Star of Our Lady). (H. R., à F., March 12, 1990).

Testimony of Sergej Grib, a Russian Scientist

"My name is Sergej Grib, married, with two children. I am from Leningrad. I am a specialist on Earth atmosphere, but I am also interested in the problems of science and faith.

Why did I come to Medjugorje? I had heard about it. I saw a film at the house of a friend who later became a priest. Those days I was in Austria. I met Cardinal Franz Koenig. He invited me to go there. I said to him:

—But I am an Orthodox!

And he:

—I beg of you, go there! There, you will certainly have the opportunity to see and experience very interesting events and even the apparitions.

"My impression was stupendous. My first impression was that one finds the answer to all the questions in the world. I felt a little alone since I was probably the only Russian in Medjugorje. But as soon as I returned, I spoke about it with my friends.

"I will go to Patriarch Alexis of Moscow. I will try to write about this phenomenon. It is easy to speak to Russians about peace, for our people desire peace. These events are a great help for all those who are looking for God. The first vital truth is that God is more real than anything else in this world. He is the source of everything and everyone, and I am convinced that no one can live without Him. No one. God gives us such joy that we cannot compare it to anything in the world." (Interview published in *Sveta Bastina,* Yugoslavia, reproduced by *Medjugorje Torino,* August 1990).

Maria Gracia Masala of Cagliari

"The Lord and Mary woke me from my sleep today at age 32. Why? During all these years my goal was comfort, and hatred and envy towards those who had more. I wanted to be like them.

"Now all of that has been locked up in a casket of which I have thrown away the key. I am not looking for comfort even if the Lord gives me the possibility of living comfortably. I do not hate anyone, but I have learned to forgive. Finally, I am not jealous of others any more, because my treasure is greater than every other, whatever may be the number of zeros which would multiply the number. I spent years finding the treasure, although He has always been the desire of my heart. I wish everyone to find this treasure in Christ and His Blessed Mother Mary." (Testimony published in *Eco* no. 77, November 1990).

Ex-Rock in the Night at Krizevac

"On the evening of Saturday, September 15, Feast of Our Lady of Sorrows, I isolated myself on Mt. Krizevac. At the end of the day, a group of friends and I made the first station of the Way of the Cross, then...we 'let ourselves go.' At a third of the distance covered, I knelt down toward the unforgettable church of Medjugorje: it was the hour of the apparition (7 p.m.). I had a feeling of solitude, and, at the same time, of indescribable communion. I relaxed as I observed the very beautiful panorama—even if, unfortunately, it is cluttered with shops and varied construction. The silence was tainted by a stereo at full blast from unknown origin [...]

"About 11 p.m. I was all alone on the large hill. I wanted to sing, but I did not do it. Interiorly I cried with joy to be there. Who would have imagined when I was in the ballroom where it seemed to me that the world stopped there? How good Jesus and Mary are for having showed me freely the world of conversion and of reconciliation. After I finished my prayer, I climbed into my sleeping bag behind the cross where there is a bench. Some people came [...]

"Toward midnight there began a real feast: a coming and going of young people who made the nocturnal Stations of the Cross. A small group of Renewal in the Spirit (with whom I wanted so much to establish contact!) arrived first with an elderly priest. After having given thanks to Jesus and Mary and calling on the Holy Spirit at the large cross, the priest blessed us with oil, and all of us who were there had a very sweet experience.

Here is mine:

"Under the impetus of the blessing, I seemed to fall backwards without being able to confront it and to enter, little by little, into a sleep of the spirit. Then, as if I were in the inside of a diving suit, I was conscious of my person but could not move anymore. I heard everything, but it seemed that I was in contact with something else or someone outside of the world. It is difficult to narrate this peace, this communion with the cosmos, during these moments or minutes, I don't know! [...] All the experiences seemed commonplace and inappropriate.

"Immediately after, I experienced the need for a general confession and for burying my entire past." (Testimony of Ante Passerini, in *Eco,* November 1990).

Ante expresses well the experience (confusing for those who see it externally) of repose (slain) in the Spirit. He tells us that he resisted it at first. And when he abandoned himself to it, he received peace, detachment, and deep relaxation, lucidity toward himself and the profound need to go to confession.

One of Numerous Vocations Born in Medjugorje

"Seven years ago I went to Medjugorje almost by chance. I was a fourth-year student at the Univesity, I was 23 years old, with the best possibilities of work and integration into the world. But, having returned home, I experienced a very strong desire of a total consecration in the religious life and the priesthood. I left everything. I entered a monastery and, by the grace of God, I have been a priest today for 20 days (October 20, 1990). Two days after my priestly Ordination, I returned to Medjugorje through a play of various circumstances, as though the Mother wanted me to reinforce the ring which She had opened here, or rather affix Her seal on this vocation. My heart overflowed with joy during all the days that I spent there. I cried to Her my thanks. To me it seemed almost a dream of being able to be here and to celebrate the Divine Mysteries.

"To the young people who listen to the same mysterious call in Medjugorje, I say:
—Do not be afraid to thrust yourselves into it. Do not look at what you are leaving, but what you are gaining, because if you thrust yourselves into it, you will end, completely straight into the arms of Mary, the Most Blessed Virgin, who will never leave you.

"Our Lady of Medjugorje continues to call. Why not listen to her?" (Dom Serafino Matteo, Community of Children of God of Don Divo Parsotti, Settignano, FE Italy, *Eco,* December.)

An Expert on Spirituality Discovers the Holy Spirit

This testimony was given by Daniela Galeazzi to some priests during their retreat:

"It was my first experience in Medjugorje. I went with beautiful thoughts in my head, beautiful convictions; I recalled the beautiful evenings spent with friends where we spoke of spirituality under every form and in all religions. By talking, I was convinced that in me spirituality had become a living, real thing. I felt superior because I had "understood" many things. Medjugorje destroyed all that and showed me the true face of the Spirit and of spirituality. My contradictions, my confusion exploded. I felt lost for a moment, but I was not lost at all because after the chaos came order, clarity. I know now what I must work on in me; what I must change and what I must cultivate. Even for prayer, it was a new experience for me. For 34 years I had lived far from God, from the Church, from priests toward whom I had strong antipathy.

"Here I prayed for the first time. It was not easy; it was even very hard for me. To pray for hours, listen to all the sermons on the Stations of the Cross without speaking, it was a real torture. I laughed bitterly at myself while discovering my limitations and how easy it was to stay behind. It was a challenge, perhaps my first challenge. Immediately, in spite of the difficulties which I had, I succeeded in penetrating the meaning of prayer; I perceived its power, its strength. I do not want to forget it. At home also I want to commit all of my strength to pray. Everyone says that I have a very strong personality, that I have a lot of energy, and all this energy I had only scattered, aimed in the most negative way which a human being can live.

"I touched the bottom: the meaning of death, the darkness in my life. But now I am happy because I discovered the other side of the coin. I understand it: life is joy and prayer is its sap. And then I discovered another unknown and criticized dimension. It was my meeting with the priests. Before this experience, I had a very negative image of a priest. For me, he was any functionary, something well defined, distant, incomprehensible, and here it was, the great discovery. Behind their black habit, they were men who lived with their strengths and their weaknesses. It was a marvelous discovery [...]. They gave me a great strength during the Way of the Cross. They were twice my age, and they climbed the hill as they calmly prayed. And I, who painfully climed behind, watched them, and I gathered strength. Thanks to these priests. If they did not exist, it would be necessary to invent them. (*Eco*, December 1990).

An Alcoholic Cured in Medjugorje

The *Medjugorje Messenger* published the testimony of a young Irish alcoholic who did not want to give his name according to the rule of Alcoholics Anonymous to whom he is today committed.

"In 1988, I came to Medjugorje for the first time. My life was a disaster. Alcohol had made me lose my trade, my health, my family, and my friends: everything. I did not go there to pray, but others took me there for it. I was happy, thinking that it was a magnificent region where alcohol was exquisite. And I drank... One evening I was, I don't know how, on the hill of the apparitions. I was alone. The night was calm and the moon bursting. I was seated on a rock. Then a thought came to me:

—Why not reflect a little on my life?

"For the first time, after many years, I felt that peace was possible even for me. From the morning of the following day, I began to look for a priest, and I went to confession.

"Now I am free, but I must be careful. In the morning when I get up, I fall on my knees and pray: Oh, Lord, help me today to give up the first glass; give me the strength to do it, and I will do the rest.

"Now I am a man, a happy man, and I can help many others. I found health again. Not my family yet. I have a son whom I have not seen in seven years, because my wife left me because of alcohol. I pray for them now and I hope. I got my job back. I pray each day for all those who have abandoned themselves to alcohol. I would like to see them free also. Lord, help them!

"Today (autumn 1990) here I am in Medjugorje to thank Our Lady, who has worked this true miracle for me." (September 1990, *Eco.*)

Two Protestant Theologians in Medjugorje

Two Protestant theologians came to Medjugorje in the autumn of 1990.

—"We came to see what was taking place here, to reflect on our Protestant position on the role of Mary."

"Are we right to exclude her," they asked themselves. "Is it appropriate to include her as much as Catholics do?" They met the visionaries, attended the apparition, spoke with priests, and participated in the liturgical celebrations. They judged the experience beneficial without delivering more precisely their conclusions.

Fifty Deaf-Mutes on a Pilgrimage

In the autumn of 1990 a group of 50 deaf-mutes made a pilgrimage to Medjugorje with a priest who was also a deaf-mute. They prayed together with gestures of a monitor standing in front of them. One evening he made them climb to the altar where they said the "Our Father" with the other faithful. They concluded:

> We will return. We have learned here what it means to believe and to pray. It will be easier for us from now on to carry our cross and our handicap of hearing for those who badly use words and for those who do not know how to give thanks for the gift of hearing and speaking. We will offer our crosses for this intention.

A beautiful illustration of the prophecy of Isaiah 35:6: "The tongue of the mute will cry his joy."

The Healing of Nicolo Pacini
(On the Feast of the Immaculate Conception, 1990)

Alberto Bonifacio, director of *Radio Maria,* twice met young Nicolo Pacini, 13 years of age, who suffered from muscular dystrophy, and whose life had changed between these two meetings:

"I had observed Nicolo Pacini on the morning of December 8 in Tihaljina, when he entered the sacristy to say hello to Fr. Jozo. I made him sit down because he walked with difficulty.

"I saw him again in the church at Medjugorje Sunday, December 9, in the afternoon, and I asked him what had just happened to him. He wanted the interview to take place outside before the statue of the Blessed Virgin located on the esplanade of the church. It annoyed him, for its was drizzling, and he had only one pair of slippers since he had left on his pilgrimage without daring to think that he could one day wear shoes. But Nicolo held to it, and it was before the statue that he gave me the following statement which I have recorded for *Radio Maria:*"

> "My name is Nicolo Pacini; I live in Ponte a Cappiano, hamlet of Fucecchio, province of Florence. I was born on November 13, 1977. I have just turned 13.
>
> "I suffered from grave muscular dystrophy *(dystonia musculorum deformans)* which should quickly lead me to death. It is a very rare illness. One of my hands always remained closed, and I could not walk. It began four years ago with a twisted foot *(piede torto);* then, in May of that same year, 1986, I got to the point of not being able to walk anymore. After that, it affected my other foot, then my hand. The other fist was also clenched.
>
> "The other week [November 28], a lady came to my house and spoke to me about Medjugorje [. . .] She had not shown me a picture of the statue of the Blessed Virgin (before which we are standing), and yet I saw it in a dream, all white, only slightly different. I also saw the statue which is at Fr. Jozo's church. She seemed to be saying: Come, come! She said nothing else. I awakened and decided to come to Medjugorje.

"Friday evening, December 7, we arrived here at the church. It was very beautiful; there was no light and there was a great spiritual recollection which one cannot find except in darkness. [...] I listened with great attention to the prayer in progress. In fact, it was the Mass, and then it happened: my right hand, which had been closed since May, opened itself very slowly. I came out of the church with the hand completely free, and I moved it perfectly. I was in my wheelchair, but my hand was cured.

"The next day, Saturday, December 8, 1990, about 9 o'clock in the morning, we returned here to the church, and I told my friend who had spoken to me about Medjugorje of the dream which I had had of this statue. We went to see it in the garden, and I took two souvenir pictures. At that moment I felt the desire to get up. I got up and everything was normal. I walked and now I am truly well."

"I spoke with Nicolo's mother (who was very emotional)," added Bonifacio. "I also spoke with the priest who accompanied this group, Fr. Giovanni Checchi, from the convent of the Redemptorists of Modena, who was giving thanks...

"Four days later, Nicolo, having landed in Ancona from the *Palladium* ferry, climbed and descended the quay of the port under the astonished eyes of the sailors who had helped him five days previously to climb on board and enter his cabin, carrying him in their arms because the wheelchair was larger than the doors." "Nicolo could not then take a step," wrote the newspaper *Resto del Carlino,* on December 12, 1990.

"His classmates (with the Sulpician Fathers from Empoli) remained open-mouthed on his return to class; elsewhere the instructors and he had a party. Nicolo remained the same, as if nothing had happened. The doctors said that there had been no possibility of a cure. The only hope was an operation of the brain, which is done in America, but with uncertain results: 'He never prayed for his cure,' confided his mother, but he always repeated:

—Where the doctors do not succeed, I am sure that Jesus will!

Testimony of Fr. Abraham

"I was born in Jerusalem of a Jewish family of 15 children, and I was raised according to the Jewish religion. Right from the start, a burning question haunted me: Who is the Messiah?

"During the last world war, in a prison camp, I bought a Bible for the price of ten cigarettes. On meditating on the New Testament, I discovered that Jesus was truly this Messiah that I was waiting for. After the liberation, I was baptized and admitted to the major seminary of Monastere de la Dormition in Jerusalem. Then I studied theology in Italy, in Belgium, and in Germany, and I became a Catholic priest. Do not call me a converted Jew, for I believed in God from the start, but after my illumination, I am no longer waiting for the Messiah. Like St. Paul, I am a Jew who no longer has a veil over his eyes, an 'enlightened' Jew.

"The light of Christ shone over me when I truly understood the word: 'I have not come to abolish the law but to fulfill it.' (*Matt.* 5:17). In Judaism we have to observe some 640 commandments. God alone can free His people with respect to the law. And Jesus came to give us a unique law which exceeds all laws: the law of Love...

"Some day the veil of all my Jewish brothers will fall. As we wait, God is faithful. He never denies whom He has chosen. St. Paul tells us: 'All Israel will be saved!'

"As I see what is happening in Medjugorje, I say to myself: The God of our fathers has had pity. He is about to shorten the time of our exile. Israel has returned. The 'New Jerusalem' descends, straight, directly from Heaven.

"Medjugorje is the greatest miracle in the world! Medjugorje is a second Israel. Mary, the Mother of God, comes there each day (for almost ten years) to speak to us of the essential. Since I heard about Medjugorje, I knew about it and believed it. Mary is the mother of all and the Queen of Peace. She comes to help her Son to save this world which is in terrible distress. To all the pilgrims of the Earth I would like to proclaim: Open your eyes and your ears...fall on your knees...and give thanks to God." (*News of Medjugorje,* March 1991.)

Pilgrim Bishops and Words from the Pope

Msgr. Michael D. Pfeiffer, Bishop of San Angelo (Texas), who let us know of his conversation with the Pope in 1986 *(Latest News #9),* expresses these most recent impressions:

"My retreat in 1989 was a pilgrimage to Medjugorje in order to pray, meditate, reflect, and learn about the great happenings in this small Yugoslav village. It was inspiring and enriching. People come to Medjugorje not as to a tourist attraction, but simply because they are looking for God and a meaning to their life. Medjugorje is a holy place, a village of Mary. Through Mary the people approach Christ and center their existence on the Gospel. [...].

"I am convinced that Mary is appearing there. [...]

"Mary comes to us in Medjugorje as an amiable and loving mother to invite us to do what her Son told us to do. If we listen to her, Christ through His Spirit will give new and admirable signs of His Grace in our works, our families, our communities, in the whole world" (translated from *Medjugorje,* autumn 1990).

Msgr. Sylvester Treinen, Bishop of Boise, Idaho, USA, stated in his homily at the Conference at the University of Notre Dame (USA) on May 14, 1989:

"During our visit *ad limina,* I had 15 minutes of private conversation with the Pope. I told him then:
—I am just returning from Medjugorje. Some beautiful things are taking place there.

The Pope answered:
—Yes, it is good for the pilgrims to go to Medjugorje, to pray and to do penance. It is good.

It is first-hand; I heard it with my ears."

Msgr. Murilo S. Krieger, Bishop of Florianopolis, Brazil:

"The Pope told me:
—Medjugorje is a great center of spirituality.

He spoke to me in Portuguese" (letter of February 24, 1990, in *Eco,* November 1990).

Msgr. Ange Kim, President of the Korean Episcopal Conference, Bishop of Su-Wen:

"During the last synod in Rome, the Korean bishops were invited to dine with the Pope.

—"Thanks to you, Poland has been able to be freed from Communism" (we said).

—The Holy Father: "No, not because of me! It is the time of the Blessed Virgin, as she said in Fatima and Medjugorje."

—The Archbishop of Kwang Ju: "In Korea, in the city of Naju, there is a Blessed Virgin statue which weeps."

—The Pope: "And there are some bishops, as in Yugoslavia, who are against . . . but one must also see the crowds who respond, the numerous conversions. All that is within the framework of the Gospel; all these events, we must study them seriously." (*Catholic Weekly of Korea,* reprinted by *l'Homme Nouveau,* February 3, 1991).

This encouragement follows suit to the words of John Paul II to Msgr. Hnilica (quoted in *Latest News #9*).
—If I were not the Pope, I would have already been there.

PILGRIM BISHOPS IN MEDJUGORJE
(Autumn 1990-Spring 1991)

—Msgr. Serafino Spreafico, from Grajau, Brazil.
—The Irish Episcopal Conference, June 11-13, 1990, recognized the great good which pilgrims draw from Medjugorje. They concluded: "Pilgrims can go there freely with private organizations. Priests can go there, not as organizers, but to provide spiritual and pastoral help necessary for the pilgrims" (*Eco,* September 1990, no. 75).
—Msgr. Anthony Salan a Puran d'Agua (unspecified country).
—Msgr. Dmyterko Stefan, Benedictine, Bishop of Stanislau, Lithuania.
—Msgr. Irénée Bilyk, his auxiliary, long time a clandestine bishop, stopped three days in Medjugorje.
—Msgr. Stanley Joseph Ott, Bishop of Baton Rouge, Louisiana, USA, remained in Medjugorje a whole week, participated in the concelebration of Mass at the shrine.
—Three prelates from New York: John Woolsey, Joseph Dispenza, and Peter G. Finn (*Eco,* October 1990, no. 76, p. 3).
—Msgr. Antonio R. Tobias, Bishop of Pagadias, Philippines.
—Msgr. Gabriel Gonsum, Ganaka, Nigeria, presided over the Mass of the place of pilgrimage (which was translated into Croatian).
—Msgr. George Speltz, Bishop of St. Cloud, Minnesota, USA.
—Msgr. Silvester Treinen from Boise, Idaho, USA.
—Msgr. André Richard from Bathurst, New Brunswick, Canada.
—An apostolic nuncio has wished to remain anonymous as

several bishops elsewhere; one of them, well known in the Roman milieu, declared "to have been struck by grace" on the hill of the apparitions (*Eco.* November 1990, no. 77, p. 3).

—Five bishops were in Medjugorje October 6, 1990: one from Canada, three from the United States, and one from Mexico (report from Fr. Orec, November 17, 1990, p. 3, who does not give their names).

Our Chapter 3 and the chronology mentioned the most important visit of three Yugoslav bishops who presided at the Mass in Medjugorje and preached there, thus officially taking over the worship:

—Msgr. Komarica, President of the Commission of Inquiry, October 21,
—Msgr. Marin Srakic, Auxiliary Bishop of Dakovo, November 5-7,
—Msgr. Janko Spenecec from Subotika in Serbia, November 24-25 (*Eco,* no. 78).

PERSONS IN MEDJUGORJE

—October 7, 1989: May Akonobi, wife of a Nigerian statesman, with her retinue.
—October 27, 1989: José Fernandez, Ambassador of the Philippines to Belgrade, with his wife and her retinue.
—October 30, 1989: the chief of the tribe of an Indian reservation in Canada with some pilgrims from his tribe.
—April 10, 1990: Denis de Concini, Senator from Arizona.
—May 10, 1990: Mary A. Harman, President of the Brazilian Red Cross and Vice President of the International Red Cross, with Stefa Spiljak, President of the Yugoslav Red Cross.
—July 8, 1990: Dr. Hans Feiff, Ambassador of the Federal Republic of Germany to Belgrade, with P. Guntermenn, coordinator of the Catholic Secretariat for the Exterior near the Episcopal Conference of Bonn.

—September 17, 1990: visit from a minister of Work and Social Service from the Federal Republic of Germany with representatives of the Federal Government of SFRJ.
—October 2, 1990: Fernando Collor de Mello, President of Brazil, with his wife and members of his state delegation.
—Prince Hans Adam II of Liechtenstein came to Medjugorje to consecrate his people and his country to the Queen of Peace (*News of Medjugorje*, December 1990, p. 5).
—September-October 1990: Mrs. Eunice Shriver, President Kennedy's sister, traveling with her husband, Sargent Shriver, former ambassador of the United States to France. They spent three days in Medjugorje while conversing with the Franciscans and the visionaries.

Chapter 7

MESSAGES

October 25, 1990, to Maria:

> *I call you to pray in a special way and to offer sacrifices and good works for the peace of the world. Satan is strong and tries with all his strength to destroy the peace which comes from God. Thus, dear children, pray with me, specially for peace. I am with you.*
>
> *I desire to help you with my prayers and to lead you on the path of peace. I bless you with my maternal blessing. Do not forget to live the messages of peace.*

November 25, to Maria:

> *I invite you to do works of mercy with love and through love for me, for your brothers and sisters, who are also mine.*
>
> *Dear children, everything that you do to others, do it with great joy and with humility toward God.*
>
> *I am with you, and from day to day, I offer your sacrifices and your prayers to God for the salvation of the world.*

December 25, Christmas Day, to Maria (the Blessed Virgin repeats seven times the word "peace". . .which has become so frequent in her message since July 25, a few days before the invasion of Kuwait and the Gulf crisis):

> *I invite you in a special way to pray for peace. Dear children, without peace you cannot appreciate the birth of the Child Jesus, either today or in your daily life. Pray then to the Prince of Peace so that He may protect you with His mantle and*

that He may help you to understand the greatness and importance of peace in your hearts. Thus you will be able to spread peace from your hearts to the whole world. I am with you and I intercede for you before God.

Pray, for Satan wants to destroy my plan for peace. Be reconciled with one another by your life in order to work so that peace can reign over the whole world.

Monday, December 31, to Ivan on the hill of Podbrdo:

Dear children, this evening your Father invites you very especially to go to church with joy [for the vigil of the young people on the threshold of the New Year]. *In the church, remain in prayer with joy and pray especially for peace.*

Ivan stated that the Blessed Virgin was happy and contented before this crowd of young people. She blessed them.

January 25, 1991, monthly message to Maria:

Dear children, today like never before I invite you to prayer. Your prayer should be a prayer for peace.

Satan is strong and wishes not only to destroy human life, but also nature and the planet on which you live. Therefore, dear children, pray that you can protect yourselves through prayer with the blessing of God's peace.

God sent me to you so that I can help you. If you wish to, grasp the Rosary. The Rosary can do miracles in the world and in your lives.

I bless you and I stay among you as long as it is God's will. Thank you that you will not betray my presence here, and I thank you because your response is serving the good and the peace. Thank you for having responded to my call.

February 25 to Maria (during the Gulf war, but on the unexpected threshold of the cease fire):

> *Today, decide for God; I invite you to it, for your withdrawal from God comes from a lack of peace in your hearts. God alone is Father; thus approach Him through your personal prayer and then live the peace in your hearts. Thus peace will be able to flow in your hearts like a river in the whole world. Do not speak of peace, but make peace. I bless each one of you and each of your good choices.*

March 18, anniversary message to Mirjana:

> *I am happy that you have gathered in such numbers. I wish that you would gather often for a common prayer to my Son. What I desire most is for you to pray for my children who do not know my love and the love of my Son. Help them to come to this knowledge. Help me because I am your mother to all.*
>
> *My children, for a very long time, I have invited you to prayer here in Medjugorje. And I will continue because I wish that you would open your heart to my Son to permit Him to come and fill you with peace and love. Permit Him; let Him enter. Help Him by your prayers so as to become able to give peace and love to others, for it is very necessary now for you at this time of struggle with Satan.*
>
> *I have often said to you: Pray, pray, for it is only through this means of prayer that you will escape from Satan and from all evil which comes with him.*
>
> *My children, I will pray for you; I promise you. But I expect from you the strongest prayers and I wish that you would spread peace and love as I have been asking you here in Medjugorje for already ten years. Help me and I will pray to my Son for you.*

March 25, Holy Week, to Maria:

> *Even today I invite you: live the passion of Jesus in prayer and in union with Him. Decide to give more time to God, Who has given you these days of grace. For that, dear children, pray and renew in a special way the love for Jesus in your hearts. I am with you and I accompany you with my blessing and my prayers.*

April 1, Easter Monday: nocturnal vigil, a little before midnight. During this apparition, as in the majority of those which take place each Monday on the hill of Crnica and each Friday on that of Krizevac, the Blessed Virgin said only the usual words: *Praised be Jesus Christ* when she arrived. *Go in peace, my dear children,* when she left. Between the two, she prayed for all people present and especially for peace in the tense situation in Yugoslavia.

April 25, to Maria:

> *Dear children, let your prayer be a prayer of the heart. I invite for each of you to find some time for prayer and in order to be able to discover God in prayer.*
>
> *I do not wish for you to speak of prayer but for you to pray. Let each of your days be filled with prayer of thanksgiving to God for life and for everything else. I do not wish for your life to be spent in words, but glorify God with works. I am with you, and I thank God for every moment spent with you.*

May 25, to Maria:

> *Dear children, I invite you, all of you who have listened to my message of peace, to carry it out in your heart, seriously and with love. Among you,*

many think of doing very much in speaking of the messages, but they do not live them.

Dear children, I invite you to life and to change everything that is negative in you so that everything may be transformed into something positive and into life. Dear children, I am with you and I wish to help each of you to live and, while living, to be a testimony of the Good News.

I am here, my children, in order to help you and to lead you to Heaven. In Heaven, there is the joy from which you can now live Heaven here below.

June 25th, to Maria:

Dear children, today, on this great day which you have given to me, I desire to bless all of you and to say: These days while I am with you are days of grace. I desire to teach you and to help you walk on the path to holiness. There are many people who do not desire to understand my messages and to accept with seriousness what I am saying.

But you, I therefore call and ask that by your life and your daily living you witness my presence. If you pray, God will help you discover the true reason for my coming. Therefore, little children, pray and read the Sacred Scriptures so that through my coming you discover the message in Sacred Scripture for you. Thank you for having responded to my call.

July 25, to Maria:

Dear children, today I invite you to pray for peace. At this time, peace is threatened in a special way, and I am seeking from you to renew fasting and prayer in your families. Dear children, I desire for you to grasp the seriousness of the situation and that much of what will happen depends on your prayers and you are praying a little bit. Dear children, I am with you and I am inviting you to begin to pray and fast seriously, as in the first days of my coming. Thank you for having responded to my call.

August 25, to Maria:

Dear children! Today also I invite you to prayer. Now as never before my plan has begun to be realized. Satan is strong and wants to sweep away plans of peace and joy, and make you think that my Son is not strong in His decisions. Therefore, I call all of you, dear children, to pray and fast still more firmly.

I invite you to renunciation for nine days, so that with your help everything I wanted to realize through the secrets, which began in Fatima, may be fulfilled.

I call you, dear children, to grasp the importance of my coming and the seriousness of the situation. I want to save all souls and present them to God. Therefore, let us pray that everything I have begun be fully realized.

Thank you for having responded to my call.

Letter to the world from Medjugorje:

PRAY AND WORK FOR PEACE IN CROATIA
Appeal from Medjugorje to all the peace centers and prayer groups inspired by Medjugorje:

Dear friends!

We rejoice with you, because through your centers, prayer groups and communities, Our Lady's messages of peace are spread to the whole world.

It is by now ten years that the messages have been traveling around the world and winning over the hearts of millions of people. People who wish to work for peace and who try to make it a part of their lives and then spread it to the others. We are certain that Our Lady has already put wonderful peace movements into motion in Europe and the whole world. She continually asks us to pray for peace: She asks that our prayer be live, intense, decisive and courageous—a prayer that can change people's hearts, change human relations within families, between people, peoples and nations.

Unfortunately, however, the peace is threatened in many parts of the world. I am sure you are all aware that just recently some regions of Yugoslavia, like Slovenia, Croatia and Kosovo, have become stages for war. Bosnia and Herzegovina also risk being involved, and Medjugorje is part of this region. For some weeks now in the Croatian Republic blood is being spilled, fear is becoming widespread and innocent citizens are being persecuted. Their houses are being destroyed by bombs. More than 100 people have already lost their lives, and more than 1000 have been injured. Tens of thousands have been forced to leave their homes.

We are asking you, dear friends, to be united with us in a more intense prayer for peace for Croatia, Slovenia and Bosnia and Herzegovina, and for all those other places where human rights and freedom are being repressed. Even though we firmly believe in the efficiency of prayer and the intercession of the Queen of Peace, we also feel it our duty to look for other means or paths that can help in any way this peaceless situation.

Therefore dear friends, who are devoted to the Queen of Peace, we also ask you to make your voices, your prestige, be heard by your governments and politicians so that all the means in their possession may be used to put a stop to this foolish spilling of blood as soon as possible, and that they help in finding a pacific way out of the institutional and political crisis that has come to divide peoples and sovereign states—whose only desire is to be united to the democratic advancement of Europe and the developed world.

Just talking about peace and negotiations is not enough. Decisive and positive help is needed in stopping blood being spilt, and to ensure peace, freedom and democracy.

We would like to express our gratitude for the help that you will give us through your prayers. We are convinced that you will be even more generous and fervent in helping us with your prayers and support, so that the peace that Our Lady incessantly calls us to here at Medjugorje, may once again be felt by us and the whole world.

We greet each one of you and we will remember you all to the Queen of Peace! Medjugorje, August 1991.

The priests, visionaries and parishioners of Medjugorje.

(Signatures follow.) (Translated from Croatian by Fr. B. Hechich.)

Message of September 25, to Maria:

> *Dear children, today in a special way I invite you all to prayer and renunciation. For now as never before Satan wants to show the world his shameful face by which he wants to seduce as many people as possible onto the way of death and sin. Therefore, dear children, help my Immaculate Heart to triumph in the sinful world. I beseech all of you to offer prayers and sacrifices for my intentions so I can present them to God for what is most necessary. Forget your desires, dear children, and*

pray for what God desires and not for what you desire. Thank you for having responded to my call.

In September of 1991, grim news from Croatia began to be disseminated around the world. The horrible atrocities that started to become evident are not included in this printing. But, perhaps The Blessed Virgin Mary summed up the situation in profound simplicity in her monthly message of October, 1991. It was the shortest message ever given in Medjugorje and didn't include the usual ending of, "Thank you for having responded to my call."

October 25, to Maria:

Dear children: Pray! Pray! Pray!

Chapter 8

CONCLUSION

The stage of this tenth anniversary is that the shrine, unceasingly attacked by false news and poor intepretations, is recognized and actually overseen by the Yugoslav bishops. Whatever be the strangeness of the communique, from the compromise which they published on November 28 and would have preferred not to publish, one can conclude with Fr. Slavko:

> "With this visit the president of the Commission removed from the priests and the pilgrims the label of insubordination which had hung over their difficult and patient obedience for a long time."

Where is Medjugorje heading? What is important is not the suspense concerning the revelation of the ten secrets or the nature of these secrets. No, it is the progression of a message in lives.

That is Medjugorje. A teaching of Our Lady. Beyond our ideologies, our systems, our administrative ideologies, our preconceptions, false appearances, and our abandonment, Our Lady continues to touch lives (and that is the reason for the prolonging of the apparitions); a triple task, which is destined to rebuild the Church inwardly, through life and faithfulness. The three objectives of the message are placed on three complementary and convergent axes:

1. Spiritual growth of the visionaries, the parish, the pilgrims, and the whole world. Today Medjugorje constitutes a world phenomenon of renewal: prayer, fasting, vocations, Christian initiatives and responsibilities.

2. Reconciliation and peace in the world. This peace is carried out first of all in the hearts and inwardly. It is the fruit of the spiritual growth. Medjugorje has assumed enough importance so that this message may be heard.

President Reagan was sensitive to the message of Maria in December 1987. Ivan's contacts with the White House (November 1990 and January 31, 1991) contributed to develop prayer which became a dimension of national life in the United States. The days of prayer requested by President Bush on February 3, later a triduum in March, were indeed prayers for peace. There was even a speech by an Iraqi during the breakfast of prayer of January 31 in Washington, where President Bush was present with some hundreds of congressmen.

It was only a minor sign among others of the movement of prayer which is developing, but also of the difficult progress of peace which the messages did not cease to promote at all levels in spite of the work of Satan who captures men in their own snares. We do not intend to canonize these efforts of prayer. Prayer is a difficult achievement, as is its perfect union with God and God's plans.

3. Widely ecumenical overture, very new because it invites beyond the ecumenism of dialogue to an ecumenism of love which will only attain the goal established by Christ: "That they may be one as We are One" (*Jn.* 17:29). This unity can only be accomplished through faith and through the heart.

After ten years the progress is striking: Medjugorje, an insignificant village, far from all the centers of communication, this place of pilgrimage which had been contested for a long time, is establishing its way. Why are so many people from throughout the world, including bishops and heads of state, drawn to this unknown spot on the map? Why, as they arrive from whatever sources, even by reading a book on Medjugorje, do they change their lives, do they find the faith again? Why are so many initiatives and so many vocations germinating? It is a mystery; it is a sign. The important thing is to live it. This message actualizes the Gospel for our times.

Chapter 9

DOCUMENTS

INTERVIEWS OF THE VISIONARIES AND OTHERS

In *Latest News #9,* we included a number of interviews, mainly of the visionaries. Here are others. We prune where the questions are without interest and where the visionaries repeat what they have already said many times in previous interviews.

MARIJANA VASILJ
(August 23, 1989)

Marijana, along with Jelena, belong to the second generation of visionaries who see with the heart. Jelena has given numerous interviews, for she expresses herself easily. This is Marijana's first published interview.

Question: Marijana, when did the Blessed Virgin begin to speak to you?

Marijana: In March 1983, for the first time.

Question: Can you remember how it happened?

Marijana: I remember it well. You know that Jelena heard the voice of the Gospa before me. We prayed with her every day. That lasted for two or three months. One day I did not come to pray. I had accompanied a friend to her house. Then Jelena came to tell me: The Gospa wants you to come to pray. It is on that day that I heard the voice of the Gospa for the first time. And since then, I hear it almost every day.

Question: What do you feel when the Mother of God speaks to you?

Marijana: It is an impression, an inspiration, like a voice from our conscience. In contrast to the six visionaries, we are not in ecstasy. We find ourselves in a very normal state. When the Gospa speaks to us, we experience a deep peace and a love which comes to us from the inside.

Question: When can you hear the Mother of God, does it matter when or at specific times?

Marijana: Only in prayer.

Question: Always or only at certain times?

Marijana: Not each time that I pray, but at least three times a week, when the Gospa gives the message to the prayer group. The Gospa also gives us messages for ourselves (personally) or for others.

Question: You have mentioned the prayer group. The Mother of God has called you and Jelena to form a prayer group. Do you remember how?

Marijana: The Gospa transmitted to Jelena the desire that we form a prayer group for young people. We were not able to do it by ourselves because then we were only 10 or 11 years old. We transmitted this desire to Fr. Tomislav Vlasic. The priests announced it publicly, and the young people followed. That was the beginning.

Question: How many prayer groups were formed here, thanks to the Mother of God?

Marijana: First of all, our group was formed; secondly, Ivan's prayer group; and thirdly, the group which Fr. Slavko currently directs.

Question: There is also what is conveniently called the little prayer group; the one which is formed around you and Jelena. Does this group always get together? What mission did it receive?

Marijana: The small prayer group gets together once a month, but all its members also belong to the large group [the one that meets in the basement of the presbytery]. The messages for the small group are the same as those which are given to the large one. As we consider the messages, we see that from message to message, the Gospa always invites us to abandon ourselves to God, to prayer. She wants us to be like a light to all—also an example for all those who come to Medjugorje.

Question: Through whom did the Mother of God give the messages of the large prayer group which meets three times a week in the presbytery? Whom does she give them to now?

Marijana: At the beginning, the Gospa gave them only through the intermediary of Jelena. But after a certain time, she also gave the messages to the group through my intermediary. I receive this message before the meeting so that one can read it at the beginning. It is read before prayer. At the end, Jelena receives a message of blessing.

Question: What is the goal of this prayer group?

Marijana: We, the young people, must pray together, live together, learn how to pray, learn to live according to our faith, and bring us closer to God. The Gospa gives us complete freedom to choose what we want to do in life. But we must give the first place to prayer.

Question: Marijana, do you hear only the Mother of God or do you see her also?

Marijana: Most often I hear her. Occasionally, I also see her with an interior vision. I never see the Gospa with my eyes [an experience in this respect different from that of the six visionaries, who see her with their eyes and can touch her].

Question: To what does the Mother of God call you and the prayer group, and what messages does she give you?

Marijana: We have often said it: these messages are a call to prayer, to abandonment to God. But the Mother of God asks us to be examples for other groups by our lives, and to see Jesus in each person, to perceive what is good and not only what is bad, and to orient ourselves according to what is good. That is what she asks of us. She says that she has come not only to help us, but also to help the whole world. I think that we can cooperate with this plan through our prayers, our example, our lives.

Question: The Mother of God always invites you to pray. How much time do you yourselves devote to prayer? What do you recommend to those who meet in prayer groups?

Marijana: The Mother of God has asked us to pray, if possible, three hours each day. Sometimes I do not get to pray three hours, but I do it as often as possible. The Gospa has stressed the importance of morning prayer. She says that we must begin the day with God. There are days when I pray less than three hours, days when I pray more.

Question: How do you spend your daily life, especially

when you are not in school?

Marijana: After we get up, we say the morning prayer as a family. Then we go to the work for which we are responsible, but often I spend my time with the pilgrims who come. After that, when I have time, I pray, then I go to church. Our group meets to pray three times a week after Mass.

Question: Has the Mother of God given messages through you and through Jelena for the whole parish or for the world?

Marijana: In the past there were some messages for the parish and for the world. But the Gospa asked the prayer group to remain close, and since then, the messages remained within the group.

Question: What do you think about the evolution of the current situation in Medjugorje?

Marijana: I think that for sometime recently a phase of luke-warmness has entered. It manifested itself, beginning with myself, for prayer and for other things. The Mother of God has called us to remain on the path where we were at the beginning of the apparitions, that is to say, to find again the fervor of prayer. We should not turn toward material things too much. The Gospa has the greatest desire that prayer take the first place in our lives.

Question: What do you recommend to people who come to your home and want to speak?

Marijana: The Mother of God tells all those who come here to Medjugorje to open their hearts. They must try to give themselves totally to God. Everything they feel and experience here, they should take back to their homes, and when they return to their home, they must be examples for those who do not believe or pray. When they return to their homes, they must continue to pray and to fast. It is very important.

Question: Has the Mother of God led you to Jesus?

Marijana: The Mother of god told us that each prayer must be a conversation with God. We can receive Jesus as our friend, as someone who is very near to us. And we must be united to Him through prayer. Particularly important must be prayer of the heart. Everything that we live, all our problems and difficulties, we should give them to God, give them to Jesus. The Gospa invites us to pray unceasingly before the Cross. She says that we must accept the Cross with love.

(This interview appeared in the English edition of *Gebetsaktion,* first trimester, 1990, and in *Stella Maris,* October 1990.)

MARIA PAVLOVIC
(February 21, 1990)

Question: It has been a long time now that the Mother of God has been appearing to you. What do you say about this period?

Maria: For me, it was purely a period of grace [...]. Day after day the Mother of God encourages me, and I experience each one of her messages like a new lesson which she gives me.

Question: How do you experience the daily meeting with the Mother of God?

Maria: Every meeting is always a great joy, ever since the beginning [...]. At each apparition, we feel something new; we do not get to be satisfied with the Gospa. Each meeting, we really wait for her with the same impatience, with the same joy. We perceive that the Gospa always gives us more; she understands us always better. She is a true friend.

Question: If, on some evening, at the hour of the apparition, you did not have the time, what would be the reaction of the Mother of God?

Maria: I do not know [...]. For the Mother of God, we always have the time, for in us she has taken the first place after God. We are always hungry and thirsty for God, for the Mother of God. In this meeting, we feel ourselves intimately committed through this freedom which the Gospa has left to us.

Question: How do you live the moments which follow the apparition?

Maria: The meeting during the apparition is a great joy.

Indescribable, inexpressible. It is truly something great. The meeting with the Gospa is a great joy for us; it is a joy which lasts even after the apparition. We are grateful to God for having chosen us.

Question: Do you feel that you have changed after the apparition?

Maria: Certainly, that is what we observe each time since the beginning. The Gospa guides us; she leads us to truth. She leads us in a special way; she always helps us to better discern the secrets of God, the path of holiness on which we are called.

But at the same time, we see our lives as they are, and many things remain as they are. The members of my family, my friends, always see in me as the same Maria. And yet, they expect from us that we set an example by our life. On one side it is a great responsibility, but on the other, a great joy, because what God gives us, we experience it like a gift. It is His will that we act through this gift. It is also a great joy for us to see that our parents and our friends entrust to us their problems and their difficulties in order to recommend them to the Mother of God, to the Gospa. [...]. It is a great thing, for we are nothing; we are only instruments of the Gospa. She uses us if we are willing. She always says: "You are free; I bow before the freedom which God gives you." And it is indeed that which we experience. God and His Mother leave us free. It is then important that we decide for God, that, in freedom, we decide to live the messages...and that we bear testimony as much as it is possible.

Question: Specifically, in what way has your life changed or not changed? How has it developed since you met the Mother of God?

Maria: I have grown interiorly during these years with the Mother of God, that's for sure. I often look at my life, beginning with this experience; it has become profound. It has also become more difficult than that of friends of our age [...]. I see a great difference when I compare them to us visionaries. It is evident that God has guided us, that He guides us [...]. The Gospa has chosen us so that we may bear testimony and unceasingly decide for God [...].

Question: Last year you gave yourself completely to the Mother of God. How do you see that for the future?

Maria: Here we do not have to say more about the private life. Many people conduct themselves in a shameless way, uncivilized, one could say [...]. Often people think that we are doctors and that we can do everything. Many think that we have opened a warehouse in order to sell good health. Even if we do not have anything to offer, many people expect something from us. We have only to offer what the Mother of God says: to live the messages, to pray, to fast. The Mother of God has said that through prayer one could even prevent wars. We can report her intentions, but she expects us to grow in the faith.

The people regard us as saints. They do not understand that we are ordinary people. We feel absolutely like the others, like everyone, like all mankind. We go through all the temptations, the difficulties, the joys which the other young people know. But at the same time, we recognize the gift which God has made to us.

Question: Many sick come to you. What does the Mother of God say about that?

Maria: The Gospa wants us to pray [...], for them to accept the messages, begin to realize them in their lives. The Gospa has often said, "Pray and fast," but there are people who are not willing to pray and to fast. It is still the only possibility of recognizing the grace which God destines to us. It is only in prayer that we will be able to really discern what is taking place in Medjugorje. One can talk about the events in Medjugorje, have a program, be theological, or it doesn't matter what else, and yet not accept the messages. These are very simple: to pray, to fast, to live in the simplicity of the Gospel. Many say the messages of the Gospa always repeat themselves! But I feel in my heart that the Mother of god loves us very, very much; she wants to save us. Salvation comes only through prayer and through fasting. We must live the messages which she has given us these many times. I am convinced that the Mother of God loves us more than herself. She wants to save us; she wants to encourage us. She wants us to change our lives. The Gospa desires that we pray, and God will act in His way. He will help us. If we do not pray, how would God be able to help us? How will He be able, if we are separated from Him, if we do not want to accept Him?

Question: You certainly meet pepole who do not want to accept suffering. What does the Mother of God say?

Maria: He who cannot accept suffering, let him offer it to God, said the Gospa. Suffering is transformed at the moment when one is ready to make the sacrifice. It is no longer a burden; it becomes a joy.

Question: Has the Mother of God spoken to you of this joy; has she spoken to you of people who are looking for a meaning to their suffering?

Maria: The Mother of God has often spoken to Vicka about it. She has encouraged her, for she had, for some time, a suffering which she could not understand. One can discern the greatness of God in suffering and the difficulties which one endures. One can know the joy which God gives. Moreover, if we do not accept suffering, we will not be able to discover the joy which is found in it. We cannot understand the meaning of it. In order to experience the greatness of God, it is very important that we pray [...].

Question: Has the Mother of God ever said anything to you on the matter of the religious life?

Maria: These recent times especially, the Gospa has often called us to pray for those who have consecrated themselves to God [...]. She desires that all those who have consecrated themselves really take the life which they have chosen seriously, and that they live their consecration.

The Gospa has said that we, too, the laity, must consecrate ourselves to God and that along with the priests and religious, we must all consecrate ourselves to the hearts of Jesus and Mary. The Gospa desires that each one of us consecrate himself as he wishes and that he especially live this consecration. We must each day make the gift of ourselves.

Question: Has the Mother of God recommended to you

to pray for special intentions?

Maria: ...So that the Will of God may be done in all her plans.

Question: How does the Mother of God personally lead you? How does she guide you in your spiritual life?

Maria: As visionaries, we each have a particular vocation, a particular responsibility. Each one of us can say it. Thus she gives through my mediation the message of each month. But she first of all asks me to live it and then give it to the whole world. I experience each message as something very strong and very demanding. But if I want to live them concretely, I can do it. The Gospa asks us to give God the first place in our lives, but often we fall back on little things. We think that we have granted the first place to God, and we immediately observe that He takes second place. That is not what the Gospa wants. We should always give the first place to God. That is what the Gospa desires of us.

Question: What does the Mother of God want from the pilgrims?

Maria: She calls all of us to live the most important messages, those which she has given many times: peace, prayer, conversion, fasting, penance, the Holy Mass. Those are the principal messages. The Gospa desires that each one of us live them. What will our decision be? Will we agree completely or semi-agree to her messages? It is certain that it will depend on us.

Question: Do you have a recollection of a particular experience with the Mother of God these recent times?

Maria: These recent times, the Gospa is often happy. She wishes us to pray! It is clear, but she is happy if we have the will for it. She knows our faults, our difficulties, concerns, our handicaps to live the messages. But the Mother of God understands all that, for she is really a mother.

(*Stella Maris,* February 1991.)

JAKOV COLO
(April 2, 1990)

Question: Jakov, do you always have the apparitions each day?

Jakov: Yes, but very recently, I had been 10 days without an apparition. They have just begun again, the day before yesterday [March 31, 1990].

Question: Why did you not have any apparitions for ten days? Did Mary tell you anything about that?

Jakov: The Gospa recommended to me to pray for ten days for her intentions and I obeyed her wishes.

Question: You said yesterday that no one is authorized to be present during your apparitions. Is it true that the Mother of God speaks to you of the secrets?

Jakov: Yes, it is true.

Question: Is the Mother of God happy with the spiritual evolution in Medjugorje?

Jakov: I do not really know. The Gospa did not say that she was happy. I think that she is happy with people who come here, pilgrims who are converted. But she is not completely happy. She is happy when someone comes here to pray, but I think that too many sins are still committed in the whole world. During an apparition I saw the Gospa cry. She said that there were still many sinners who offended her Son with offensive remarks.

Question: When did you have this apparition? A few days ago?

Jakov: No, some time ago, almost a year ago.

Question: Where do your apparitions take place?

Jakov: It depends, but most often at home.

Question: When you are not at home, do you always have apparitions in the evening? They say that the place does not matter.

Jakov: Yes! Always there, where we are. We always have the apparitions at the same time.

Question: Currently can you ask questions of the Mother of God?

Jakov: Not now; I cannot ask anything.

Question: How was it during the time when you did not have any more apparitions?

Jakov: It was difficult and a little strange because for a long time I had apparitions without interruption, and then they were interrupted. Before, I had them every day.

Question: How does your daily life unfold; what do you do?

Jakov: I work at the parish. But nothing special. After work I return home, and there if I need to give a helping hand, I do it.

Question: You often meet with pilgrims. Do you notice a change in them in comparison to those who were there two or three years ago?

Jakov: I do not know. Pilgrims are always what they are. [...]. I cannot judge. For the most part, it is new pilgrims, new groups, who come.

Question: In her last message, the Mother of God told you that we are not really conscious of what her coming means. You see her every day. How do you live all day in the presence of Mary?

Jakov: During the day I am careful to spend as much time as possible in prayer. The Gospa asks it of us, and also to live her messages. It is only for that, I think, that she has said that we do not have enough awareness of her presence, for if we were aware of it, we would realize her messages and what she has said.

Question: Can you be more specific? What seemed the most important?

Jakov: I have already said it. It is the messages which the Gospa repeats to us almost daily: prayer, conversion, peace, penance, fasting, and the Holy Mass.

Question: How do you get to do penance, to fast? Do you have any problems?

Jakov: I admit that at times it is difficult. But if one does it with love, nothing is difficult. At times, I too have days when I cannot. For the Mother of God has told us that Satan wanted to turn us away from her plan and prayer. Satan wants to dissuade us, but we must defend ourselves.

Question: A personal question: when you have committed a sin, are you afraid of the apparition of the Mother of God?

Jakov: When I have committed a sin here or there, there have been some cases in which the Gospa has told me how I had sinned.

Question: Are you especially afraid, for example, when you have done something bad and you fear that the Mother of God will discover it?

Jakov, a little embarrassed, repeated and finally answered:

Jakov: I have never done anything serious; nothing which would have really justified fear.

Question: If you had a reason to fear, would it be painful to meet the Mother of God?

Jakov: My meeting with the Gospa is always the same. The question of knowing whether we experience fear seems to me superfluous. It was the case during the first apparitions. But now we experience a very great joy from day to day. If one compares the current apparitions with the first, they are not different.

Question: Would you be able to describe briefly for us how you see the Mother of God? How does she come? Do you also see the heart, the cross, and the sun?

Jakov: Before the apparitions, we see the light three times. Then the Mother of God appears and greets us with a *Praised be Jesus Christ*. Previously we would ask her our questions. Now we recommend to her all the sick, we say an *Our Father* and a *Glory Be To The Father*. When the Gospa leaves, the cross, a heart, and a sun appear.

Question: If I understood correctly, you pray with the Mother of God when she comes.

Jakov: Yes, and I recommend to her all the people who have come.

Question: How do you see the light?

Jakov: I do not know the nature of this light. It is neither white nor yellow. I cannot explain how it is.

Question: Do you see at times the Mother of God praying for us and for the people?

Jakov: Yes, the Gospa blesses us also every evening, us and all the people who are present.

Question: Does the Mother of God come with angels? Have you yourself seen any sometimes?

Jakov: Yes, but not very often, only sometimes.

Question: At Christmas how does the Mother of God appear?

Jakov: On great feast days she appears dressed in a golden dress. And it is thus that she comes at Christmas with the Child Jesus.

Question: Have you seen the Child Jesus?

Jakov: Yes.

Question: Have you seen the Child Jesus only or the Mother of God who is holding the Child Jesus in her arms?

Jakov: Yes, the Mother of God was holding Him in her arms, like one carries a little child.

Question: These last times, has she said anything to you about the secrets?

Jakov: Yes! Yes! She began again to speak about them yesterday.

Question: Has the Mother of God told you anything on the subject of changes which are taking place in the East?

Jakov: To me personally, no.

Question: How do you see your mission, your responsibilities insofar as a visionary is concerned?

Jakov: The Mother of God did not take away our freedom. She leaves us free in everything. We do not have any particular responsibility.

Question: And yet you have the grace to see the Mother of God. Do you draw any responsibility from it?

Jakov: The Gospa wishes that we transmit her messages. I do not think that it is an obligation. It is through love that we do it.

Question: Many people have their eyes fixed on the visionaries. They judge you in a positive or negative way. What do you think about it?

Jakov: We are people like others, normal people. I think that I conduct myself normally, like all the others. I desire to be like the boys of my age. Not in everything, but in certain things. When my friends invite me to coffee, I find that completely normal, even if it makes more than one person talk.

Question: The Mother of God made you see different things. Has it been possible for you to see Paradise?

Jakov: Yes.

Question: What did you see?

Jakov: I do not want to speak about it. It was a personal experience; I do not want to say anything about it.

Question: Your father and mother are dead. How have you carried this cross?

Jakov: It is true that I did not overcome everything all alone, but one can succeed at everything with the help of the Gospa. She helped me with it.

Question: You see the Mother of God every day. What is your relationship with Jesus? Has it been modified, deepened with time? What is there for you?

Jakov: I do not really know what I should say about it. In fact, nothing has changed. I love Jesus as previously, but I have had contacts with the Gospa for a long time.

Question: How do you live the Holy Mass?

Jakov: I experience it as the heart of our life, and I strive to do my best to live it always more profoundly.

Question: The apparitions will come to an end some day for you as for Mirjana and for Ivanka. Is the Mother of God preparing you for that moment or rather is it still unthinkable?

Jakov: I do not know anything yet. Nothing makes me sense it, nothing.

Question: Do you have any presentment of this great sign about which they speak so much? Is it still with us?

Jakov: She promised this sign, and we know when it will take place.

Question: The Mother of God desires the formation of prayer groups. Are you also in a prayer group, or do you pray alone?

Jakov: Yesterday we had prayer here. All of us who work here at the parish pray together. It is not a special prayer group, but we pray together.

Question: Do you think that for people who work together it is necessary to pray together also?

Jakov: Yes, we should pray together, for the Mother of God recommends to pray together, especially in families or in groups. We who work together are like a little family.

Question: What relationships do you have with the other visionaries?

Jakov: We are a little scattered. Each one has his work. But in spite of all, we see each other often.

Question: How do you see your future?

Jakov: I do not wish to speak about it. I have not yet made any particular decision.

Question: What would you recommend to pilgrims who come here for a second trip?

Jakov: I have already said it: to live the messages as the Gospa recommends.

(This interview appeared in English and in French on September 30, 1990, in *Stella Maris*. The name of the interviewer was not seen in either of these two editions. The French interview seemed a translation of the English, but more wordy.)

MARIJA DUGANDZIC
(Autumn 1990)

Marija Dugandzic, 24 years old at the time of the interview, has exercised a very great influence on prayer groups in Medjugorje. For a year she was in the community which Tomislav Vlasic had founded near Vicenza. She remains an "external" member of it after events scattered or divided the community to a certain extent. Then she worked at the Atlas Tourist Agency. She is currently working on her licentiate in theology in Rome.

Question: Marija Dugandzic, you are part of Jelena's prayer group. Do you want to talk to us about it?

Marija: With this prayer group we have grown and learned very much; we follow a school of prayer. Through the six visionaries, the Gospa speaks, gives messages, and guides us. Through these girls, Jelena and Marijana, she helps us to put into practice what she says.

To this prayer group she presents herself truly as a mother, and in all the meetings, she has given us a message adapted to the circumstances. She does not give a message for each person, but for the group, and we travel together. She has also always wanted for us the presence of a priest to explain the word, the message. For four years we had Fr. Tomislav. Now, we do not have a permanent priest, particularly because they are truly very busy in the parish.

Question: How many times do you meet, and how do the meetings develop?

Marija: We meet as a group three times a week, but at least once there is one of the priests with us. It has already been more than seven years that the Gospa guides us in this manner through these two girls. The Gospa did not give them secrets, as she has done for the visionaries. She did not speak of events, but through them she has wanted to guide us to deepen our spiritual life; that is to say, to truly live with the Lord the whole day. The Gospa has indeed repeated this invitation many times: *I desire that your life become prayer.* She has made us understand that all things which are part of our life can be offered as prayer. To live with the Lord means to offer Him *everything,* but we will not have the courage and the spirit to offer everything if we do not also practice prayer as a time devoted to the Lord. She asks us for prayer, but she also asks us to participate in the Holy Mass, not only on Sunday.

Assuredly a path is necessary. Everything cannot be accomplished from one day to the next, but the Gospa calls us to a decision and often repeats: *Decide for the Lord.* It undoubtedly seems to us a little strange that after all these years, she still says, "Decide." But once she reproached us and even yesterday she said: *"You are surprised because I say to you: Decide for God. And yet, see how you have lived this day!"*

We want to live at the level of the spirit, and we say that we have decided, but when we examine our attitudes, we see that it does not correspond. The Gospa wants to take us to this life where we "will experience" the Lord Himself in our behavior and not only when we pray. She wants for the life of the spirit and the life of the body to be a unique life, offered to the Lord, given to the Lord as He gives it to us.

The Gospa has also made the following reproach to us before God: *You often have an egotistic attitude.* Once after Christmas, two years ago, she gave us this message: *Dear children, in these days you have prayed very much, but your hands have remained empty.* And she gave us a theme about which the group must dialogue. For the Gospa wants that, beyond prayer, we have each week a group interaction over our experiences. This evening she asked us to comment on this theme while each one responded to the question, "Why have I remained with empty hands?"

We understood what the Gospa wanted to tell us. Many of us were looking for other things. We had our requirements, our intentions. And during that time, Jesus was born, He wanted to give Himself to us. And we looked for something else: odds and ends, while He wanted to give Himself completely.

Question: Can you give us some advice?

Marija: When you return home, ask yourselves the question: "How is it that I act, it seems to me that I already have my hands and my heart closed...I do not know how to act." The Gospa told us at the beginning [the group hardly started]: *If you want to do something, do it in your family.* We thought of doing something, something for the world, but let us begin with our little world in being faithful to the Lord. And He will use us as instruments. We do not know even how. In fact, the Gospa has said: *The fruits, leave them to the Lord, do not worry about anything or anyone but entrust yourselves to the Lord.*

Question: On an average, how much time do you devote to prayer?

Marija: That depends. In the group we usually pray an hour and a half. We have meetings three times a week, in the evening after Mass, and each time the Gospa sends us a message. We see that the message of the Gospa is related to the Gospel of the evening. Constantly she invites us to the

Gospel: to read the Gospel, live the Gospel, as if she wanted to detach us from what she tells us while quoting the words of Jesus Himself in the Gospel: we will never be without the Word! She wants to teach us to live with the Word of God and does it in her maternal way.

Question: Do you meet here in this room to pray?
Marija: No, in the parish.
Question: How many are there in your group?
Marija: Some twenty, thirty...
Question: What does the Gospa recommend for families?
Marija: Above all, pray as a family. Pray together. The Gospa recommends union with God. Thus all the problems will be put in their place. If together we find time for God, there will be no more problems and if there are some, we will know how to act because the Lord helps us.

(Translated from *Medjugorje Torino,* November-December 1990.)

IVAN DRAGICEVIC
(November 1990 at the meeting in Herndon [Virginia, USA])

This interview was published in the *National Catholic Register,* Supplement *Mary's People,* January 27, 1991.

Question: What should one do for members of the family who do not believe?
Ivan: Be an example for them and pray for them.
Question: Ivan, can you explain to us why the apparitions are shorter now than at the beginning? Can we be present when you have an apparition here in the United States?
Ivan: The apparitions are shorter—between 5 and 8 minutes. I do not know why. While I am here, the apparitions are private, only for the families where I stay.
Question: What is the best way to receive a complete healing?
Ivan: We must pray for the healing. God can be glorified through a healing, but we must accept the will of God.
Question: What were you doing at the time of the first

apparition?

Ivan: I was playing ball. [He did not state precisely the time or the day. It was June 24, 1981, where he gave only a glance at the first and distant apparition and ran away.]

Question: Has Our Lady said anything about the crisis in the Middle East?

Ivan: Our Lady did not particularly speak about the Middle East, but she has asked us to pray for peace and we know that we must do it when peace is in peril. We must really accept that prayer changes the course of things, for Our Lady has said that with prayer even wars can be prevented.

Question: Do you encourage a trip to Medjugorje? Can we accomplish the same thing here in the United States?

Ivan: The messages of Our Lady can be heard in the United States. The people who go to Medjugorje have the experiences. They experience the presence of Our Lady in a very special way; they receive peace. The people with whom I spoke said that they had a very special experience. Some pilgrims told me that they go to Medjugorje to find peace and to pray better, and they are filled with it for their return home. People go to Medjugorje to renew their faith. It is their goal. Some go there in order to find Our Lady; they go there for God. Some say that we go there to pray to Our Lady and that we abandon Jesus. No, it is not true. We pray to Jesus and we go to Him through Our Lady.

Question: Has Our Lady mentioned anything about abortion?

Ivan: Our Lady has spoken about abortion to Maria and Vicka, and during these last two years, she has spoken to me also. She has told us to pray for this intention.

Question: Will Our Lady leave a sign at the end of the apparitions?

Ivan: Our Lady has promised to leave a sign in Medjugorje when the time comes, but now it is we who must be the sign. Our Lady has given messages to Maria for our Holy Father and they are going to be delivered to him.

Question: One has attributed to you that a sanctuary would be built in 1982 or 1985 in Medjugorje on the hill of the

apparitions. It did not occur. What do you say about it?
Ivan: It is the first time that I heard anything about it.
Note: Actually, the question was inspired by the fact reported in *Latest News #4*. On May 9, 1982, two members of the Commission had compelled Ivan, then in difficulty at the minor seminary, to write the secret. Ivan, intimidated, had written and placed under seal, some lines which were not really the secret. He wrote particularly: "The Blessed Virgin will leave a sign. There will be a large sanctuary in Medjugorje." etc. Since Ivan said later that he had not written about the secret in the sealed envelope, the Commission opened this envelope on March 7, 1985. Ivan does not seem to have established a link between the question asked here and this painful event in his life.

Question: Has Our Lady spoken to you about St. Joseph and about the Child Jesus?

Ivan: She has not spoken to me about them, but at Christmas she comes with the Child Jesus.

Question: Are the people of Medjugorje called to a special suffering? Is there a special invitation to pray for them?

Ivan: Some responsibilities weigh on the parish of Medjugorje. They also have crosses to bear. The visionaries are joyful and happy with the messages from Our Lady, but they also have their responsibility...Look at the events which have taken place for nine years. The greatest event is the conversion of people, the renewal of spiritual values in the world, a return to the Church, return to the faith. The questions which you ask are good questions. The most important should be what she gives us. It is good to hear how Our Lady considers everything that occurs, but the messages, her messages are the most important thing. She tells us to pray and then we can live the messages and everything becomes clear for us. That is why I say: accept prayer, accept the messages and everything will be clear for us. I have prayed for peace, and we can see the changes which have taken place in the world today. Today we always ask when Russia will be converted, but no one asks: "When are we going to be converted?"

Question: A question was asked concerning the smell of roses. Has the Blessed Virgin said anything regarding this matter?

Ivan: It is wonderful to smell the roses. It is pleasant when everything smells good.

Question: Why did Our Lady choose you?

Ivan: For nine years I have asked myself that question.

Question: Did Our Lady tell you anything about "Evangelization 2000" and about the coming of her Son Jesus?

Ivan: An evangelization has begun toward the Second Coming, I cannot say anything.

Mirjana and Ivanka have ten secrets and they see Our Lady once each year. Vicka, Maria, Jakov, and I myself have nine secrets. I cannot speak of the secrets since they are secrets. The secrets will be revealed when the time comes [...]. I cannot speak of Hell and of Purgatory. I have only been to Heaven [in spirit and vision...].

Question: What does Heaven look like?

Ivan: When and if you go there, then you will know. But we do not seem to ask which is the road to Heaven.

Question: What were your feelings at the time of the first apparition?

Ivan: During the first six months, it was a great shock in our lives. But now the shock has sweetly diminished. I must say that I am more free to speak to Our Lady than I am here [to speak with you].

Then as they adjourned the session, Ivan ended by saying:

Ivan: I ask the young people to return to God and to commit themselves really to prayer and the rosary. And I ask the parents to assume their responsibilities and the priests to help them. The priest should be the shepherd of your life.

JELENA VASILJ
Interview by Sofia
(November 30, 1990)

In this transcription, we extract only some more personal or less known elements.

Jelena: Everything began for me a year and a half after the beginning of the apparitions. I was ten and half years old. It was at school that I heard the voice of an angel. Fifteen days later, this voice made room for that of the Blessed Virgin. Three months later, Mirjana had the same experience: some messages from the Blessed Virgin, then from Christ.

The Blessed Virgin wanted us to form a prayer group which began six months after the first experience. [...] After the formation of the group, she confided some messages to us, practically at each meeting. That took place about 8 p.m., after the evening Mass. Our meetings lasted from an hour to an hour and a half. She asked us to seek the training of a priest or spiritual guide.

What the Blessed Virgin expected from each of us was our response and our spiritual growth. If each one of us was not sufficiently ready to evolve, to develop himself spiritually, the group would not have any chance for growth. The essential is prayer, the point of departure. The Blessed Virgin asks us to address God directly, while experiencing Him, by profoundly living His presence. If we know how to live Him, experience Him in our prayer, then we will be able to recognize God in each of the others, in each daily situation.

Recently the Blessed Virgin requested that we pray very much for peace. She recommended silence:

If you speak unceasingly in your prayers, how will you be able to hear God? Allow Him room to answer you, to speak to you.

She recommends to pray for all those with responsibility in the Church and in the political world, for all those who have special gifts, but who do not know how to recognize them.

This year I am preparing for a [nursing] degree at the school in Mostar. The trip takes half an hour to go, half an hour to come. I have to find the time for prayer and the prayer group in the family chapel which you see there. Those who do not have the opportunity to go to Mass come to pray with us in the morning before leaving for work or in the evening when they return.

Fasting on bread and water? I have experienced this call to self-denial, and through this detachment from material things, one discovers freedom. I will not say that I fast each time.

Contacts with the six visionaries? We do not have them often. We are not of the same generation; we did not see each other regularly before. And the visionaries themselves have a difficult time getting together once a month, they are so busy. But we participate in their meetings on the hill. Our experiences are different from theirs: locutions with visions through the heart, no apparitions.

The condition for the locution? It is not like when you are walking. It does come all at once. The condition for the locution is deep prayer; it can hardly have taken place in school. Sometimes at home, generally in the church at the time of meetings.

Question: Is the group closed?

Jelena: A certain discipline is necessary in this kind of group, which took a four year commitment to form, so that all would be willing and develop together. If each one goes and comes haphazardly, growth of the group is impossible. Certain members of the group have left it in order to go elsewhere, into religious life or to get married, but few other persons have joined us. In order to receive other persons, it would be necessary for them to be ready and willing to commit for a certain period of time.

Question: Have you received messages about the Gulf war?

Jelena: The Blessed Virgin does not speak of the countries, but of people. She appeals for prayer for peace, but it is a general appeal.

Question: Are there any Muslims in your class?

Jelena: The Muslims whom I know admire Medjugorje. Some would wish even to join our faith, but for them the problem is tradition, another system of education, and it is very difficult to change.

Question: In studying for your degree, how can you pray three hours a day?

Jelena: The essential thing is the decision to do so. Once we have decided for prayer, we find the time, whatever may happen and whatever one does. I do not know how to tell whether it is indeed three hours by the watch every day, but one always finds the time to pray to God.

LUDEVIT RUPCIC, O.F.M.
Excerpts from an Interview
(November 30, 1990)

Divisions produce tensions. Everything is limited. Still, God is infinite. God alone can accomplish the infinite desires of man. Christ is our peace and His gifts are beautiful. The Blessed Virgin gives us the most beautiful of gifts. Nineteen million people have come here.

For my part, in the beginning I was against Medjugorje, but now I am for it. I believed that at the beginning it was "a joke." But, when I saw these people again, I said to myself: there is something here. My book on Medjugorje surprised many priests. As a theologian, I am a little rationalistic. I am not a rationalist, but I use reason for theology. I am on my fifth book on Medjugorje.

Two hundred books have been written about Medjugorje throughout the world. It is the greatest Eucharistic table and confessional in the world. In the spring there were as many as 10,000 confessions a day, 30,000 Communions. A bishop said: It comes from the devil. The Pope quickly silenced him.

Many initiatives flow from here, or settle here. The price of land is 330 francs per square meter. They are soon going to build, six minutes from the church, a reception center with a chapel.

RECOLLECTIONS OF FR. JOZO ZOVKO (1990)
(Of Some Events of July 1981)

A Sign Requested and Received

I was alone, praying in the church. I was praying to God with all my heart to give me a valid sign in order to convince me whether the work was from Satan or from Him. Those were the days when the police made the families of the area and the visionaries, the six young people themselves, suffer. Here many had lost their jobs for having disobeyed the regulations of the police and of the government, for instead of remaining silent, they would tell everyone who came what was happening. All would suffer for defending that the Gospa was there. I, on the contrary, suffered because I did not want to believe. It was then that a strong human voice resounded in the church:

—*Go out and protect my children. Then I will tell you what you will have to do.*

Instinctively, I got up and I went to the back of the church. I opened the door on the left when, from the right, like swarming bees, the six visionaries rushed in all around me, tugging and grabbing hold of me.

—"Save us, the police are chasing us!"

I took them to the presbytery and locked them in. I went outside and down the flight of stairs and, behold, the police came running by and asked me:

—"Have you seen the young people"

—"Yes, I answered."

And they, without waiting for the rest of my answer, continued on their way. But I was still not convinced. That night I talked at length with these young people. It was little Jakov who asked me why I did not believe. I answered him:

—"Because people do not come to church and it cannot be the Gospa who keeps them away."

I referred to the curious people who came from the outside and wanted to see signs, but not to pray. It was then that Jakov told me:

—"Tomorrow people will come to the church!"

And it was thus so.

No one had told them. Before, all went to the hill of the apparitions. That day the church was full.

The Beginning of the Daily Rosary

Then the area was blocked by the police and by the army. The visionaries, controlled by the home guards, could not leave their houses. Jakov had the apparition in his home. The Gospa gave a message for him to bring to me at the church that evening for Mass. He was like a prisoner in his home, for the armed guard was in front of his door. Jakov, so small, felt that he should obey the Gospa. He looked through the key hole. When he saw that the guard had fallen asleep (for here in July it is very warm), quietly he opened the window and jumped out. The guard awakened, entered the house, and saw that he was no longer there. By radio, he informed all the stations of the blockade in the direction of the church. Jakov changed cars six times in order to escape the stations of the blockade. He arrived at the church as I was finishing Mass. I felt someone pulling on my sleeve. I looked down and saw him. He told me very quietly:

—"The Gospa has given me a message for the people."

I lifted him up and I stood him on the altar before the microphone. He said:

—"The Gospa told me to come to tell you to pray the rosary this evening."

The people immediately felt that the Gospa was near them. Many began to weep because it was a period of great repression on the part of the police. They looked for the rosary in their pockets. It was the first parish rosary which was said in the church at Medjugorje. I put Jakov back on the floor. He was barefooted, dirty and dusty. On the altar cloth remained the imprint of his two little feet. Then the Gospa came in the middle of the church and thanked me, and added the same words from Jakov:
—*You must say the rosary every evening.*

And since then, in Medjugorje, we say the rosary always.

In order to succeed in reconciling the families of the parish, always in conflict among themselves, we had three days of fasting. At the end of these three days, the word "MIR" (Croatian for "Peace") was written in the sky between the mountain of the cross and the church, with letters of fire, like a river which suddenly came toward us. It was August 6, day of the Transfiguration. We saw what looked like a flame leap from the large cross on Mt. Krizevac. We were seized with a paralyzing terror. We wanted to escape from this enormous avalanche which advanced toward us and which was burning in the sky. It was like the end of the world. But no one, did I hear say afterwards, had even thought or said: "God forgive us." No one felt the possibility of fleeing this river of fire: MIR, "Peace," this word of "peace." We understood what it meant. God wanted peace. We understood the urgency of making peace. Mary is the Mother, the Queen of Peace.

(Recollection recorded by Pietro Zorza, *Italiani in Scozia*.)

In Prison

Pietro Zorza then goes on to tell of the imprisonment of Fr. Jozo; the apparitions and strange phenomena with which he was blessed during the time of his imprisonment: locks did not lock, and mysterious lights troubled the guards and resulted in some conversions among them. I feel it would be very useful that these facts, often narrated, be confirmed today by these guards themselves who no longer need to remain silent. For lack of confirmation, one will always say that it was the golden legend.

The narrative which we have formerly recorded from Fr. Jozo, this exceptional eye witness, is basically exact. But there is much we could not confirm for it is a fact that his memory is inaccurate on dates as well as details. And Jakov has challenged the statement that he "changed cars six times" on the way from his house to the church. This information surprises him. These recollections have worth as a memory of the heart, not for its historical rigor.

LÉONARD OREC, O.F.M., Rector of Medjugorje
Report to the President of the Commission of Inquiry
S. E. Msgr. Franjo Komarica
(November 1990)

At the end of September 1989, I sent you a detailed and exhaustive report on the events in Medjugorje as I see them and have seen them. After 14 months, it seems to me necessary to do it again.

1. The Pilgrims

1.1 The shrine of Medjugorje as a place of pilgrimage continues to grow. The place is known more and more throughout the world. This year, for example, we had pilgrims from Oman, Sri-Lanka, the Island of Guam, Kenya, Peru...

1.2 One observes now pilgrims from the countries of Eastern Europe: Hungary, Czechoslovakia, Poland, Romania, Bulgaria, different republics of the Soviet Union, and also the German Democratic Republic.

1.3 The number of pilgrims has increased from 20 to 30%. We infer this especially from the number of Holy Communions distributed. The following table gives the statistics from 1985 to 1990:

Months	Communions					
	1985	1986	1987	1988	1989	1990
January	6,100	10,000	15,000	20,700	24,000	29,400
February	16,800	12,000	20,000	17,900	19,000	33,000
March	23,500	42,500	30,000	61,500	67,000	65,000
April	42,500	49,000	64,500	111,000	99,500	143,800
May	36,800	57,500	86,000	106,000	129,400	143,350
June	69,000	59,000	100,700	115,500	101,675	133,800
July	43,000	41,700	95,000	82,200	85,000	113,500
August	77,000	92,500	101,500	171,400	127,200	205,300
September	46,000	83,600	112,700	96,500	110,700	183,500
October	59,500	71,400	96,500	135,300	167,100	198,200
November	38,000	30,000	45,000	61,000	42,500	56,000
December	24,000	34,200	37,500	39,500	45,000	69,000
Total	482,200	583,400	804,400	1,018,500	1,018,075	1,373,850

1.4 Pilgrimages via foot have expanded. They come from Herzegovina, western Bosnia and Dalmatia, and also from Sibenico, Slvonca, Pozega, Ljubljana, and at times from Spain, France, and Germany. A group of 30 pilgrims, who came from Bergamo in northern Italy, arrived on April 23, 1990.

1.5 Many participants in international congresses and symposia or meetings come to Medjugorje. For example: the group of doctors from Lithuania, who came to the Congress of the Family in Zagreb; the group of experts in international law from Dubrovnik, etc. Some persons of international fame agree to give talks at meetings which are held in Yugoslavia in order to be able to come to Medjugorje.

1.6 The number of young pilgrims has increased. Beyond the international meeting of young people (which has become a tradition with as many as six thousand participants), groups of young people often arrive from Austria, Germany, Italy, and, in particular, from southern Tyrol; and others from Croatian regions. A pullman of young pilgrims from Moscow has been announced.

1.7 This year (1990), pilgrim priests are particularly numerous. Outside of those who accompany the groups, there are many groups of priests, especially those who have participated in the spiritual exercises "Evangelization 2000," at the Vatican. In September, groups of priests from Lithuania (27), from the United States (more than 100), and Brazil (51) came to Medjugorje. Already for some years, groups of Italian priests (85 today) often make spiritual exercises in Medjugorje. The statistical information on priests celebrating Masses, with respect to the nationality of priests, is not without significance:

Month	Year	Croates	East Europe	Germany	English	Italian	French	Others	Evening	Total
Jan.	1989	144	1	22	177	81	1	11	366	803
	1990	198	1	52	154	83	1	16	308	813
Feb.	1989	133	2	33	104	46	10	21	235	584
	1990	148	15	77	125	69	9	32	297	772
Mar.	1989	153	1	102	305	88	39	24	640	1,352
	1990	185	3	112	452	126	32	56	652	1,618
Apr.	1989	183	29	220	937	192	60	130	1,471	3,222
	1990	187	58	330	859	186	85	98	1,401	3,204
May	1989	207	46	203	1,016	134	132	128	1,387	3,253
	1990	247	106	186	1,467	173	172	117	1,564	4,032
June	1989	241	69	123	1,025	230	116	132	1,488	3,424
	1990	300	102	182	1,213	273	114	121	1,567	3,872
July	1989	266	121	165	531	193	59	86	1,086	2,507
	1990	287	137	163	595	224	87	110	1,088	2,691
Aug.	1989	267	228	218	944	334	83	206	1,238	3,518
	1990	298	240	168	965	457	131	163	1,722	4,144
Sept.	1989	307	84	217	1,143	249	136	113	1,447	3,696
	1990	252	109	212	1,433	334	146	262	2,345	5,093
Oct.	1989	230	62	336	1,550	211	92	154	1,778	4,413
	1990	229	101	307	1,601	232	107	190	1,954	4,721
Nov.	1989	170	10	93	536	340	28	83	1,563	2,823
Dec.	1989	171	2	57	244	67	41	14	397	993
TOTAL	1989	2,472	654	1,789	8,512	2,165	796	1,102	13,096	30,586
	1990	2,331	871	1,789	8,864	2,165	884	1,165	12,898	30,967

1.8 The number of visiting bishops continues to increase. The largest number came from the United States and from Canada, then from Brazil and the countries of Latin America. One has also seen bishops from Africa, Australia, the Philippines and India. Among the bishops from Europe the most numerous are the Italians. The Croatian bishops who come now give us a particular joy.

To cite one case, on October 6, 1990, five bishops were together in Medjugorje: one from Canada, three from the United States and one from Mexico.

1.9 It is also interesting to recall a number of distinguished personages in public and political life. Among others, some who have visited Medjugorje are:

October 7, 1989: May Akonobi, spouse of a Nigerian chief of state, with her retinue.

October 27, 1989: Jose Fernandez, Ambassador from the Philippines to Belgrade, with his wife and retinue.

October 30, 1989: The chief of the tribe of an Indian reservation in Canada, with pilgrims from his tribe.

April 10, 1990: Denis de Concini, Senator from Arizona.

May 10, 1990: Mary A. Harman, President of the Brazilian Red Cross and Vice-President of the International Red Cross with Stefa Spiljak, President of the Yugoslav Red Cross.

July 8, 1990: Dr. Hans Feiff, Ambassador from the German Federal Republic to Belgrade, with Fr. Gunter Mann, coordinator of the Catholic Secretariat for the Exterior near the Episcopal Conference in Bonn.

September 17, 1990: The Vice-Minister of Labor and of Social Services from the German Federal Republic, with representatives from the federal government.

October 2, 1990: Fernando Collor de Mello, President of Brazil, with his wife and members of the state delegation.

2. What Is It That Attracts Pilgrims?

2.1 We cannot speak of interior motives, in particular, of the work of the Holy Spirit. That belongs to Him Who enters into the minds and hearts. Many pilgrims state that an interior force drives them to come to Medjugorje. Many have been led to Medjugorje by the accounts of other people who have gone there, books which they have read, or information received through the media. Some heard of Medjugorje from tourist agencies. Some have come with friends and acquaintances or only to see what was happening in this place. Many were looking for physical or spiritual healing.

2.2 The great majority said that they came for religious motives: meeting with God, meeting with oneself, prayer, confession, the desire to change life, inspiration for the apostolate, etc.

2.3 Many say that they find more peace in Medjugorje than at home or in other places of pilgrimage. Those who received reconciliation in the sacrament of confession especially speak of peace.

2.4 One always hears of miraculous healings of people who have come to Medjugorje or in relation to Medjugorje. Some bring medical documentation of their illness and their cure.

One of the most interesting cures which took place this year is certainly that of the multiple sclerosis of the well-known singer Lola Falana from California in the United States *(Latest News #9)*.

Likewise, Antonio Piras from Sardinia, who was cured in his home from cancer and paralysis when his parish priest took him a stone from the hill of the apparitions.

Italian television, as well as the other media, spoke of both cases.

Donica Anderson from the United States is stated to have been miraculously cured after a highway accident. Testimonies of this kind come to us frequently.

2.5 The majority of the pilgrims wish to meet the visionaries and hear from them direectly of their experiences, messages and other things. At times, pilgrims can meet the visionaries in their homes. Ivanka Elez (maiden-name Ivankovic) and Mirjana Soldo (maiden-name Dragicevic) have started families and succeeded in resisting the assault of the pilgrims. Likewise Jakov Colo avoids these meetings as much as he can. Vicka Ivankovic, Maria

Pavlovic, and Ivan Dragicevic are continuously exposed to the encounter of curious but pious pilgrims.

2.6 The greatest concentration of pilgrims in Medjugorje is at the celebration of Holy Mass. It is celebrated in the morning in different languages at the church, in the chapel of the apparitions, and in the new chapel of adoration. Sometimes in the morning there are fifteen Masses in different languages. The most numerous group is the English-speaking. From the beginning of April until the end of October this group flourishes; and at times they do not all succeed in entering the church. During this time, there are from 50 to 100 priests concelebrating at Mass.

After the English-speaking group comes the German-speaking group. They too, cannot always enter the church because of the crowd.

After them come the Italians and the pilgrims from the countries of eastern Europe. The evening Mass continues to be the solemn occasion of the day. From June to October, the Mass is celebrated in an uninterrupted way on the outdoor altar with several thousand of the faithful participating and many priests. The number of priests often exceeds 100.

2.7 The adoration of Jesus in the Most Blessed Sacrament always becomes more intense. Beyond the regular adoration on Thursday from 2 to 5 p.m. in the church, and that of Wednesday and Saturday, they have introduced, at the beginning of September 1990, daily adoration in silence from 1 o'clock to 5 o'clock in the chapel built for that purpose.

Many wish for the adoration to become continuous, day and night, and we think that it will someday become a reality when the chapel is finished. This year, the youth conference on prayer, under the title "Youth 2000," was completely under the sign of the Eucharist. In the tents set up for this occasion, throughout the whole week,

2.8 **Medjugorje has become the confessional of the world.** Many come from very distant places to go to confession because, according to their statements, in their church and in their country, one does not find the opportunity. In some countries in the world, individual confession has become a rarity. In Medjugorje the sacrament of confession is available in many languages and at any time.

Some people from all parts of Croatia and Slovenia, who for years or decades did not go to confession at all for political or other motives, know that in Medjugorje they will certainly be heard. These people have been some of the numerous hosts this year. More than the *quantity* of confessions, what is stupefying is the *quality*. Life conversions are not rare.

2.9 The rosary is recited each day in the evening: Joyful Mysteries and Sorrowful Mysteries before Mass in the evening, and the Glorious Mysteries after. The hill of the apparitions has become a special place to recite the rosary together or individually. Both day and night one sees groups of pilgrims, at times hundreds, who together recite the rosary. Basreliefs (embossed images) of the Joyful Mysteries help in the contemplation of these mysteries, fundamental to the faith. Similar images of the Sorrowful Mysteries are already prepared and will be installed soon. In the spring, they think that the Glorious Mysteries will also be set up.

2.10 Mt. Krizevac has more and more become a special place of adoration of the Cross of Jesus...where groups of pilgrims make the Stations of the Cross. [...] The wooden crosses were replaced in 1988 with basreliefs in bronze at each station. To the classic stations, the artist Carmelo Puzzolo has added, at the beginning, the prayer of Jesus in the Garden of Olives, and at the end, the Resurrection. The steep path has been widened by the feet of thousands of pilgrims, who often climb with bare feet. Many of the sharp rocks of Herzegovina have worn smooth through contact with human steps.

So that pilgrims on their descent do not bother those who are climbing while praying toward Krizevac, four groups of Austrian youth, last summer, built a descending path as volunteer work.

Pilgrims, who because of old age or illness cannot climb Krizevac, are asking for the Stations of the Cross to be built near the church.

2.11 The cemeteries of Medjugorje, Bijakovici, and Miletina (the three hamlets of Medjugorje), are places where the pilgrims stop and pray. The cemeteries have been poorly maintained, and it would be better to establish a more suitable place of prayer.

2.12 A large number of pilgrims look for the opportunity to pray in silence: spiritual exercises, silent retreats. However, numerous projects for local and foreign communities have come ahead of these desires.

2.13 The sick pilgrims ask that we pray for them, with them, and over them. Scheduled prayers for the sick take place each day after Holy Mass. Besides, one prays over the sick whenever it is requested. The sick and items for the sick are ritually blessed accordingly.

2.14 Each day, the mail and the pilgrims bring hundreds of letters with prayers to the Blessed Virgin for healing or some other need. It would be interesting to study all these letters from the psychological, sociological, and theological point of view.

2.15 Many adults, especially those who have attained the faith through Medjugorje, desire to receive the Sacrament of Baptism while there. [...] We advise everyone to do so in the parishes where they reside so that they can, from the beginning, be associated into the life of the local church. Some argue for the bond between their conversion and Medjugorje, and their desire has been fulfilled. It is thus that in 1989, fifteen adults were baptized. In 1990 through today (November), there have been 12 baptisms.

2.16 Fourteen couples, not belonging to the parish, were married in the church of Medjugorje in 1989. In 1990 up to this day, 10 couples.

2.17 These recent times, special devotions tied to the sacraments have taken hold: the renewal of the promises of baptism, the priesthood, marriage, as well as the renewal of monastic vows. The experience of this celebration has aroused very much enthusiasm.

3. Pastoral Charge of the Pilgrims

3.1 All the priests stationed at Medjugorje are at the pastoral service of the pilgrims. Today there are seven. Besides the seven, some Franciscans of the (neighboring) monastery of Humac devote a great part of their time to the pilgrims. The Franciscans of adjacent parishes generously assist in hearing confessions, especially on Saturday and Sunday. Some priests from foreign countries help in the pastoral work for the foreign pilgrims in a permanent or temporary manner. The priests who arrive with the pilgrimages also help with confessions. During the summer months, actually from April to October, confessors are most often from 20 to 50, sometimes more.

3.2 Seven Franciscan sisters are stationed in the parish of Medjugorje. One of them leads the songs in church. Two work in the sacristy; two in the pastoral work of the parish. All, each in her own way, help the pilgrims. Some religious or similar communities also spend time with the pilgrims.

3.3 The members of prayer groups of the parish offer their services to pilgrims in praying with them and in helping them become oriented to the places of prayer.

3.4 Our priests and foreign priests are available not only for confession but also for other pastoral services, in particular for individual conferences. No one who desires to go to confession in Medjugorje will return home without confession. In spite of all the external assistance, we cannot either quantitatively, even less qualitatively, fulfill the spiritual demands of so many pilgrims who ask for special spiritual services, and they are always very numerous. Many seek counsel in the area of spiritual theology, mysticism, and other things. It might become necessary to have a larger number of capable priests, acquainted with the demands and problems of modern man, and who, besides general theology, know the domain of spiritual theology, mysticism, psychology, psychiatry, and other disciplines, and that they speak the required languages.

3.5 For the improvement of our priests in the practice of the pastoral, we have organized two seminars with the Slovenian Jesuits: Marijan Sef and Radogost Grafenauer, and also a seminar with Dr. Anton Penvin, professor of theology at Rijeka, with Dr. Heribert Muhlen, renowned expert and professor of theology in Paderborn.

3.6 We continue to have a weekly meeting of the pastoral staff and a meeting of our priests who help in the pastoral work in Medjugorje.

3.7 Some spiritual exercises and seminars have been organized for the pilgrims.

3.8 To our pilgrims and foreigners we offer the possibility of participating from time to time in cultural events. Among other things, the church choirs have performed: Chorus Angelorum from the United States, Bachchor by

Sindenginfen, from the Cathedral of Kaunas in Lithuania, as well as national and foreign singers. Under the direction of Jakov Sedlar, the actors of the National Croatian Theater from Zagreb have put on the comedy of Karol Wojtyla: *The Brother of Our God.*

3.9 Many groups of pilgrims give concerts of spiritual music.

3.10 This year the anti-alcoholic club which offers professional aid to those who are dependent on alcohol, be they from our country or from abroad, was begun.

4. The Material Conditions for the Pastoral of the Pilgrims

4.1 The number of pilgrims in Medjugorje is always increasing. The church can no longer hold all of the pilgrims who participate at the evening Mass. To be able to worthily celebrate the Eucharist (especially for when the number of pilgrims exceeds 2,000), an altar has been set up to celebrate outside with room for 120 concelebrants. In front of the altar, the grounds have been laid out in a terrace to hold some ten thousand pilgrims. Approximately 4,000 faithful can sit down on strong wooden benches.

4.2 The little chapel for perpetual adoration with an area of 180 square meters [...] already serves as a place to celebrate the morning Mass for small groups of pilgrims of the same language. In the afternoon, it is used for adoration in silence.

4.3 Two large and two small rooms have been built for conferences, catechesis and other activities as well as some rooms for individual conferences.

4.4 Two large tents with an area of 1,200 square meters, useful for large gatherings, have been set up.

4.5 Twenty roofed confessionals have been built on the side of the church.

4.6 We have built a large cistern with an area of 640 square meters for water reserves.

4.7 To provide a rest area for pilgrims, the grove next to the old church has been developed. On the edge of the grove, they are in the process of finishing some new resting places.

4.8 For spiritual concerts in the evening, the adjoining space by the old church has been prepared.

4.9 They have just finished a house for priests: five apartments, four rooms with a kitchen, living room and bathroom.

4.10 For the sisters, ten rooms have been built with kitchen, living room and bath facilities.

4.11 Currently, the parish house is being remodeled.

4.12 This year, we have given particular attention to the development of the project of town planning for Medjugorje and Bijakovici. To this goal, many consultations have been made with the town planners and exhibitors of the local community. The group of town planners (architects, representatives from the municipality and local communities, the Council of Churches and of the parish office) visited the sanctuaries of Lourdes and Fatima in February 1990.

4.13 Considering the experience of Lourdes and Fatima, and while taking into consideration all the specific characteristics of Medjugorje, the Institute for Town Planning of Bosnia and Herzegovina set up a plan for Medjugorje and Bijakovici. The basic concept of this regulating plan has been approved by the municipality of Citluk on October 2, 1990.

4.14 On the basis of different analyses, the basic concept foresees that in Medjugorje and Bijakovici, 56 hectares of land on which to build will be reserved for sacred places, and that Mt. Krizevac and Mt. Crnica (apparition hill) be absolutely protected from all future construction and that the current respect be maintained.

4.15 This same plan anticipates the bringing together of the church and the hill of the apparitions, the "Oasis of Peace" on Perkusa and Krizevac by means of circular routes; and that they be brought together also by little pedestrian walkways, next to the routes, and by paths through the fields.

4.16 National and foreign institutes, always very numerous, request the construction of spiritual houses in Medjugorje and Bijakovici. It would be desirable that these types of buildings be coordinated, but no one feels competent to take on the task.

5. Civil and Ecclesiastical Authorities Addressing Medjugorje

5.1 The Yugoslav civil authorities at first persecuted the visionaries, imprisoned the Franciscans, forbade access to the hill of the apparitions and Krizevac, and controlled the coming of pilgrims by taking note of their registration. They opposed every kind of construction around the church. With the years, the authorities understood that Medjugorje did not represent a social menace but, on the contrary, a help for the weakened economy. The civil authorities then began to be kind and to consider with great indulgence the coming of the pilgrims and their lodging in state or private facilities.

At the present time, the authorities maintain very good rapport, with the sanctuary and the pilgrims. In fact, recently the civil authorities have almost become completely helpless. Except for a little general order and public security, everything is pretty much out of their hands.

5.2 The helplessness of the authority is felt in their attempts to control the construction and the commerce, just as the impossibility of fighting the speculation of the economy of the country.

The roads do not correspond, even from a distance, to the number of vehicles. Telephone communications are often interrupted; the network is failing. Thus, the peril of an epidemic is serious for a country where there are thousands of people and tens of thousands of guests.

5.3 During these last two years, the civil authorities helped with the organization of large meetings of faithful: supervising the traffic, watching over public security, offering sanitation and other services.

5.4 Recently, HDZ from Bosnia-Herzegovina has included Medjugorje into its political program.

5.5 There is a certain amount of improvement in the relations between the Church and Medjugorje. This year, for example, the celebration of Confirmation took place calmly (the bishop preached the word of God without polemics). On the side of the bishop, there is no official trouble. In recent times, some contacts have been established with Croatian bishops who participate in the celebration of Mass. That makes the members of the parish, the parishioners, and the pilgrims happy.

6. *Medjugorje: A Good for the Church*

6.1 During the nine plus years which have transpired, Medjugorje has become, without any great human resources, the gathering place of pilgrims from the whole world, the meeting point of new evangelization, the international center of peace. Such development came about spontaneously without the help of civil and ecclesiastical authorities in spite of all kinds of prohibitions. The time has come to verify the current situation in order to see the opportunity and the dangers, so as to move into the future in a more concrete way.

6.2 In Medjugorje, everyone becomes one single family. Here one meets people of all races and classes, of all colors of skin and languages, and all feel brothers and sisters. The great international tensions of races, classes, faith, work, which devour modern humanity, disappear here.

The tide of pilgrims experiment with the message of peace and carry it to the world. Is it not a concrete way to bring about union among nations?

The suggestion that Medjugorje be declared an "international zone of peace" is no longer a dream or the utopia of a poet.

6.3 Many Centers of Peace, which have been formed in the world after being inspired in Medjugorje, could serve as the leaven for peace for which the world strongly aspires.

6.4 People, motivated by religious inspiration, come to Medjugorje. These people are looking for God. They are open to the proclamation of the Gospel. Is it not an opportunity for "Evangelization 2000," about which the Holy Father so often speaks? Many pilgrims in Medjugorje wish to become messengers of the Gospel.

6.5 Many young pilgrims have experienced a call to the religious vocation while in Medjugorje. Many religious and diocesan communities already have candidates and members who have come through Medjugorje. In the novitiates of the Franciscan province of Herzegovina, there are six candidates (50 percent) who have come through Medjugorje. Among them there are two Croatians, three Americans from the United States, and one Australian.

6.6 We are familiar with some religious communities which were founded through the inspiration of Medjugorje [above, pages 61-66].

6.7 Medjugorje brings together an always increasing number of priests, not only the curious and the guides of pilgrimages, but even of true "converts" who change their way of life and of work, and who devote themselves completely to the work of evangelization. A number of them, individually or as a group, make their spiritual exercises here. To these priests we should offer greater attention and more adequate spiritual help. This would be a great opportunity for evangelization.

6.8 Always more young pilgrims arrive in Medjugorje. During the summer months there are thousands. The international festival of prayer, "Youth 2000," which developed this year, has shown that the youth of today is not only enthusiastic but is capable of leading a very intense spiritual life.

6.9 Some young Austrians, as volunteer work (four groups of fifty) spent two weeks in Medjugorje in work and prayer. They have a lot of enthusiasm. For next year, it is being proposed to bring young people from other countries. Groups such as these are useful, not only to those who work, but to those who see them work, as well as for the families of the parish who give them free hospitality during the most difficult season.

6.10 Inspired by the messages of Medjugorje, many prayer groups have come into existence and arise throughout the world. They become the seed of a renewal of prayer in the world.

6.11 The pilgrims of Medjugorje show a great willingness to materially assist their brothers and sisters in need. Without hesitation, they help countries which have been struck by natural catastrophes in order to conquer sickness, poverty, etc. Many funds have been collected to help, among others, the Armenians after the earthquake; the families of dead miners in Tuzli; some sick people who had to be referred for operations. Even if it was inadequately organized, a considerable amount of help had been given (clothing, food, money) to regions in Kosovo, Albania, and other countries in Eastern Europe.

6.12 The pilgrims of Medjugorje willingly help the missionary work of the Church. Besides the important regular generosity destined for the missionaries, they also help the sisters and needy priests. Among other things, they have helped with the construction of the cathedral in honor of the Queen of Peace in Kaminika in Zaire. Now they are helping with the construction of the Franciscan house in Zaire, at Kolvezi.

6.13 The pilgrims of Medjugorje use their time in concrete actions for prenatal care. In many countries they are actively helping everything which is done toward this goal of the right to life.

6.14 The Church in Eastern Europe offers a special opportunity for evangelization. A considerable number of pilgrims come to Medjugorje and ask for religious literature in their language. Many are ready to work as apostles in their own country. Also among them, are those who are ready to preach the Gospel in the vast Soviet Union where prohibitions to evangelize have practically disappeared. The ground has been prepared. It is waiting for the seed, the sower. One has to ask himself what will take place now, and with what seed.

It is hoped that this report, though incomplete, will help the Commission and all those responsible in the Church to have a better perspective of these events, so that they will assist in seeing that the pastoral work in Medjugorje can be accomplishied without further disturbance for the greatest glory of God and the salvation of souls.

Fr. Leonard Orec
Medjugorje, November 17, 1990

ASSESSMENT OF IVAN DRAGICEVIC'S TRIP TO THE UNITED STATES
(January 31-February 5, 1991)
Letter from Congressman C. H. Smith

From: February 25, 1991
Christopher H. Smith
Commission on Security in Europe

To:
Ivan Dragicevic
MEDJUGORJE MIR CENTER
Wichita, Kansas

Dear Ivan,

I would like to take a moment to let you know how deeply appreciative Mary (wife) and I are for your faithful and compelling testimony concerning your heavenly meetings with the Blessed Virgin.

From my point of view, your visit to Washington D.C. was a success. The numerous speeches and talks which you gave provided many people with the rare opportunity to hear about Medjugorje by an eye witness.

Knowing how unbelievably full your calendar was while in the United States, I think that it can be useful to note some highlights of your visit to Washington D.C. from Thursday, January 31, to Tuesday, February 5.

At the Annual National Prayer Breakfast, where you were Wednesday morning, January 31, more than 3,000 people gathered from different denominations in order to share and to pray. A small number of government leaders spoke at this breakfast, including President Bush.

The reception in Congress, which I hosted in the House of Representatives, permitted a dozen interested congressmen and a larger number of members of their staff to hear you for two hours speak of the messages of Our Lady. You will recall that you answered a number of questions from congressmen. Some of them were skeptical, and they understood your detailed explanations on Medjugorje for the first time.

You behaved with great humility and candor [...]. You will be interested to know that your performance raised a considerable discussion about Medjugorje. [...]

[He speaks of the congressmen who were absent and continues:]

On Friday morning (February 2), you addressed the National Prayer Breakfast Youth Seminar. [...] About 125 Christian leaders participated, the majority Protestant or Evangelical. Many of them had never heard of Medjugorje and found this miracle extremely difficult to understand, so that the tone of many of their questions could appear "hostile" (sic). I informed my wife that you had a difficult task. At the end of the seminar, it is remarkable that many were not only more informed on Medjugorje but better understood the role of Mary in our lives.

The experience which you had at this seminar with the youth shows the difficulty of many non-Catholic Christians in accepting Mary as a messenger of God today. Let us hope that these young Christians will discover that to honor and to love the Most Blessed Mother is not only a "Catholic matter." After the youth seminar, you were interviewed for an hour for the radio show, *Voice of America,* by Fr. Victor Potapov. You met Mark Gallagher of the Catholic Conference of the United States (a key personality) as well as a photographer and reporter for the *National Catholic Register.*

On Saturday you met Doug Coe, outstanding Christian leader who directs Fellowship International and who is the chairman of the National Prayer Breakfast. Doug and his organization have carried the good news of Jesus Christ to leaders of government, parliamentarians, and ambassadors throughout the world. It was, then, important to meet them and discuss with them the events of Medjugorje.

For my family, Saturday afternoon and evening (February 3) were specially memorable after a great workout on the basketball court. My family, including my parents and close friends, joined us in our living room at the time when you were meeting with the Most Blessed Mother (the apparition). It was an awesome experience, a true blessing.

On Saturday you met several priests and seminarians, a distinguished judge, and another Republican congressman, Bill Lowery (R-California) and his wife for a time of prayer and reading of the Bible, followed by the apparition. On Monday you met another group of men and women, influential in Washington, including the wife of Barber Conable, President of the World Bank. My calendar prevented me from joining you, but my wife told me that you did a fabulous job, that your feelings were apparently shared by many during this meeting.

Early in the afternoon [of the same Monday, February 5], you were interviewed by the *Washington Times* [...]. Unfortunately, a number of planned meetings could not be held, especially with Christian Television (CBM-TV: Christian Broadcast Network) under the direction of Pat Robertson. [...]

As you know, the meeting with the President never came to fruition in spite of several conversations with John Sununu, Bush's chief of staff. Peggy Stanton also used her connections in order to try to arrange a meeting with the President. Perhaps some seeds have been planted for a future meeting with the President and for interviews by different secular and regular media in the United States. [...] Allow me to conclude: you were very lucky to have the assistance and support of Nives Jelic [organizer of the trip with her husband]. Mary and I think that she is an extraordinarily gifted person. She gives so much of herself in order to advance the cause of Christ and the messages of the Blessed Mother!

Christopher H. Smith

Chapter 10

CHRONOLOGY

1990

June 13: A Hungarian television team came for the first time to film in Medjugorje (*Eco* 74, p. 3).

July 25: Eight days before the occupation of Kuwait and the Gulf crisis, there was a message insisting on peace. This word was repeated nine times *(Latest News #9)*.

July 31-August 6: "Festival of Youth 2000" in Medjugorje: 5,000 participants.

August 9: Mark Chodako (USA) sent to different experts (of whom I am one) a first draft of his film script for consultation in view of a proposed major film on Medjugorje.

August 15: Prince Hans-Adam II of Liechtenstein consecrated his people and his country through Mary, Queen of Peace. His wife, Princess Maria, and her children were with him. It was not his first trip. He ended his consecration by saying: "May my country, in spite of its small size, become the kingdom of your Son, a kingdom where justice and peace reign. Guide me in all my actions and help me in each decision, so that I can carry out my responsibility properly and that I may be truly a father for your country. Amen."

August 26-29: New Festival of "Youth 2000" organized for 600 young people in Medjugorje.

September 15: Feast of the Cross on Krizevac: "200,000" faithful, said the Yugoslav radio, not without some exaggeration *(Eco.)*

September 26: Jozo Dalent, an electronics engineer, arrived in Medjugorje at the end of a trip of 812 kilometers on foot from Ljubljana, which he had left on September 1. He came to give thanks for a healing of his legs. Up to that point he could walk only with crutches. He also came to pray on the anniversary of the deaths of his wife and his son who died in a traffic accident.

October 2-3: The President of Brazil, Fernando Colar de Mello, came from Prague to Medjugorje, accompanied by his wife and his retinue. He attended Mass with Ivan and Maria. He entrusted his government and his country to the Blessed Virgin. "I have come here to renew my faith," he said. "I believe that the Queen of Peace will help me and my country to resolve all the problems which we have to face." Asked concerning the peace of the world, he answered, "Yes, peace is possible, but it depends on us; we are responsible for it, and praying is the first step toward all peace."

October 4-8: Vicka went on a pilgrimage to Fatima. She stopped at St. Lucia's convent. She left her a warm message. She denied that she was upset not to see her.

October 5-7: Maria's trip to Italy.

October 9: Mark Chodako finishes his film script and sends it for a second consultation.

October 11: Msgr. Hnilica blesses the Medjugorje Center in Vienna, in conjunction with the cardinal.

October 15: Maria leaves for Czechoslovakia and Russia where she is going to join Msgr. Hnilica, a Slovak bishop, with Fr. Orec.

October 16-17: Some young Lithuanians give a concert in Medjugorje *(Eco).*

October 21: Msgr. Komarica, President of the Commission of Inquiry on Medjugorje, came to celebrate Mass at the place of pilgrimage. He spoke for a long time in an open, positive and constructive manner with the priests and those responsible for the parish. It was a relief. "We are no longer treated as dissidents and protestors or disobedient," said one of the participants.

October 23-24: Maria in Moscow. She has two apparitions there *(Eco).*

October 24: Ivan's arrival in the United States, in Pennsylvania and then Wichita, Kansas (at the Jelic residence).

October 25-28: T. Vlasic meets some young people in Tocco da Casoria (PE Italy). My (Fr. Laurentin) twenty-fourth trip to Medjugorje.

October 26: Maria's return to Medjugorje.

November 2: Msgr. Franic's colloquium at St. Peter's

Cathedral with the recovered drug addicts of Sister Elvira, who had come from Saluzzo (Cuneo, Italy).

November 3: A 50-minute film about Medjugorje on Croatian television.

November 5-7: Msgr. Marin Srakic, Auxiliary Bishop of Dokovo, member of the Commission of Inquiry, visited Medjugorje, presided over two Masses, and gave an enthusiastic homily on the Blessed Virgin. He then visited the provincial of the Franciscans and the bishop. Thus was achieved the promise made by Msgr. Komarica: "Some Yugoslav bishops are going to come now to bring their pastoral assistance."

November 12-16: Spiritual exercises for an important group of Italian pilgrims.

November 15: Ivan sends a message of peace to President Bush. For some months the Americans had worked to get this meeting. It was not immediately determined that it took place. But it was then that the meeting of January 31 at a Breakfast of Prayer was decided.

November 17: Fr. Orec's Report to the Episcopal Commission of Inquiry: A remarkable account on Medjugorje, its acquisitions and its needs.

November 25: Msgr. Janke Spenesec from Subotica (Serbia) came to Medjugorje, Saturday the twenty-fourth and Sunday the twenty-fifth of November. He presided over two concelebrations of the Mass at the shrine and gave the homily on Sunday.

November 25-December 1: Vicka is in Switzerland.

November 27-28: Extraordinary meeting of the Yugoslav bishops on Medjugorje. Msgr. Zanic vigorously and irresistably opposes any positive statement. The assembly votes what appears to be a very negative resolution, but which leaves the question open. The supernatural was not established (but not excluded). The pastoral of the place of pilgrimage must receive the help of bishops (pilgrimages are not forbidden at all contrary to the false news proclaimed with insistence by some authorities using their influence with the international press).

December 2-21: Maria in Italy.

December 8-9: Medjugorje Conference in New Orleans, LA.

December 8: Blessing of the bronze basreliefs representing the Sorrowful Mysteries on the hill.

Mirjana enters a maternity ward in Mostar for the birth of her first child.

December 9: Birth of Maria, Mirjana's daughter.

December 10: Visit of Msgr. Josif Arneric, Bishop of Sibenic (78 years old) and Msgr. Franic, Archbishop Emeritus of Split.

December 11: Maria and Slavko promote spiritual reunions in Italy.

December 12: They are in Pescara and are interviewed by the RAI.

December 13: They are in Foggia. Ivan returns from the United States.

December 23: Blessing of the 48 bells of the right side of the belfry, and a concert of bells. At 5:40, at the time of the apparition, they play the "Ave Maria" each day.

December 28: Second visit from Msgr. Frane Franic to Medjugorje, "the vigil of his birthday"; he was born on Decmeber 29, 1912 *(Eco).*

December 31-January 1: Vigil of the youth for the New Year; prayer on the hill with Ivan, apparition at 9 p.m., and return to the church where midnight Mass was celebrated.

1991

January 2: Unauthorized publication of the communique from the Episcopal Conference (November 27-28) which the bishops intended for Rome, but not for the press, as they made it known in *Glas Koncila*. One asks himself about those who were responsible for this leak (see Chapter 3).

January 3: The Italian newspapers began the publication of the communique: "negative verdict," according to the commentary from *Asca*. After *L'Avvenire* consulted me, the authentic interpretation made its way with the support of *Radio Maria* (Alberto Bonifacio) and of *Eco* (Don Angelo).

The circulation of the communique continued the following days in the world press with the customary disturbances as in similar cases.

January 11-28: Vicka's trip to the United States. She held meetings in New York, Detroit, Chicago, and in Florida.

January 21: Ivan's new trip to the United States.

January 31, Thursday: Ivan attended a prayer breakfast, anticipated since November. Many congressmen participated. President Bush requested that the following Sunday be a day of prayer throughout the country: prayer for peace, not for victory.

February 3, Sunday: A day of prayer for peace in America at the request of President Bush.

February 5: Vicka's arrival in France with Sister Emmanuelle for a three day visit to the community of "Lion of Judah."

February 8: Msgr. Zanic meets John Paul II for approximately 15 minutes. Nothing came out of the meeting.

"In Rome, you are reported to have said that the statements from the Yugoslav bishops wanted 'to preserve Medjugorje from the fanatics and the gurus. Is this correct?' " asked the *National Catholic Reporter,* which gave the news (February 24, 1991).

"I must remain silent," Msgr. Zanic answered in substance, referring to instructions received from Rome.

February 8: Vicka held a meeting in Paris in the large room of the Mutualite: 2,000 seats, insufficient for the crowd of more than 3,000 persons which had to be in great part held back after having waited for hours through freezing temperatures.

February 9, Saturday: Vicka's second meeting with young people at the church St. Gervais.

February 10: Vicka held another meeting at Lipsheim (60 kilometers south of Strasbourg).

February 17: Slavko's departure for the United States at the beginning of March.

February 22: Jakov's departure for Regensburg (Germany).

March 6: Jakov returns to Medjugorje after a trip to

Germany and Switzerland.
March 16-22: Maria in Italy.
March 31-April 3: My twenty-fifth trip to Medjugorje.
April 10: A new communique from the Yugoslav bishops on Medjugorje. They confirm not to have evidence on the supernaturalness of Medjugorje and announce the undertaking of liturgical and pastoral responsibility of the worship.
April 26: Vicka's departure with Fr. Petar for a week in Poland.
April 28-May 7: Jakov's departure for Italy.
May 9: Vicka in Poland, Hungary, and Czechoslovakia.
May 17-19: National Convegno (Conference) on Medjugorje in Florence for the tenth anniversary with Vicka and Jozo Zovko.
May 6-24: Maria in Italy.
June 14-16: Third Medjugorje Conference at Notre Dame, Indiana.
June 24-25: Tenth anniversary of the first apparition. On this day, Ivanka has her sixth annual apparition at her home. My twenty-sixth trip to Medjugorje.
July: The civil and political crisis of Yugoslavia erupts. Croatia and Slovenia declare their independence. The dark shadow of civil war covers the country.

MEDJUGORJE

The following books of Father Laurentin have been translated into English, and are currently available from The Riehle Foundation.

The Apparitions at Medjugorje Prolonged ($5)
By Fr. René Laurentin
Update book through June 1986.
Fifth anniversary, news of the seers, scientific studies, the messages.

Latest News of Medjugorje ($4)
By Fr. René Laurentin
Update book through June 1987.
The marriage of Ivanka, response to the objections, information on the new commission.

Seven Years of Apparitions ($5)
By Fr. René Laurentin
Update book current through Fall 1988.
Sixth anniversary, the controversies, testimonies, the fruits.

Eight Years ($5)
By Fr. René Laurentin
Update book through July 1989.
Seventh and eighth anniversaries, investigations, latest messages, wonderful interviews with the visionaries.

Messages and Teachings of Mary at Medjugorje ($7)
By Fr. René Laurentin
The chronological listing of over 700 messages from Medjugorje, applicable to Scripture and Catholic doctrine. Emphasis on the urgency for the world to return to God.

Nine Years of Apparitions ($7)
By Fr. René Laurentin
The events of Medjugorje through 1989 up to September of 1990. Extensive interviews and testimonies. 240 pgs. 32 colored photos.

If you wish to receive copies, please write to:

THE RIEHLE FOUNDATION
P.O. Box 7
Milford, OH 45150

All contributions are used for the publishing and/or distribution costs of providing spiritual material to a world desperately in need of learning more about and living in God's peace and love.

THE RIEHLE FOUNDATION...

The Riehle Foundation is a non-profit, tax-exempt, charitable organization that exists to produce and/or distribute Catholic material to anyone, anywhere.

The Foundation is dedicated to the Mother of God and her role in the salvation of mankind. We believe that this role has not diminished in our time, but, on the contrary has become all the more apparent in this the era of Mary as recognized by Pope John Paul II, whom we strongly support.

During the past four years the foundation has distributed over two million books, films, rosaries, bibles, etc. to individuals, parishes, and organizations all over the world. Additionally, the foundation sends materials to missions and parishes in a dozen foreign countries.

Donations forwarded to The Riehle Foundation for the materials distributed provide our sole support. We appreciate your assistance, and request your prayers.

IN THE SERVICE OF JESUS AND MARY
All for the honor and glory of God!

The Riehle Foundation
P.O. Box 7
Milford, OH 45150